APACHE

A detailed look at the AH-64A Apache Attack Helicopter

"There is nothing to compare with it in the world. The Apache defeats twice as many targets at twice the range and does it in 60 percent of the time required by the most advanced previous attack helicopter."
Lt.Col. David Sale, Apache System Manager, Army Training and Doctrine Command

By simple definition, the AH-64A Apache is a multipurpose attack helicopter whose primary missions are antiarmor and escort in adverse weather by day or night. The U.S. Army needs a helicopter that can provide responsive and decisive firepower on call from ground commanders and survive to battle again. Apache satisfies that requirement.

Building a helicopter that could destroy tanks protected by antiaircraft weapons and also provide suppressive firepower in a variety of scenarios meant rewriting the book on attack helicopter design. Until Apache, military helicopters represented steady, measured progress in airframe-engine combinations to which weapons were added as they became available. The air cavalry concept of the early 1960s became a reality in Vietnam. However, by the 1970s, the increasing threat from ground fire alone meant that the helicopters then flying could not survive a battle in which the penetrating tanks would maneuver with antiaircraft protection. Unique flight abilities are useless if a helicopter cannot get within range to launch its weapons and survive. The modern attack helicopter may have been conceived in a sea of doubt about its ability to survive in a hostile environment against a determined, heavily armed adversary. That issue has now been settled.

In setting the specification now filled by Apache, the Army wrote a list of requirements for a machine that could operate effectively in any theater of combat, around the clock, in fair weather or foul. This new machine had to have a higher degree of survivability than ever achieved before. It would carry a greater load of more refined firepower than any predecessor. Performance, which goes hand in hand with agility and maneuverability, would have to be the best attainable or mission effectiveness and survivability would suffer. And once in the field, this new machine had to be kept flying with a minimum of maintenance.

Meeting these ambitious specifications meant advancing technology in airframe, propulsion, avionics, visionics and armament systems. Visible success has been demonstrated in the AH-64A Apache built by McDonnell Douglas Helicopter Company, teamed with the most capable aerospace companies ever concentrated on a helicopter program. Their exceptional technical resources and management abilities made it possible to design and build the Apaches now rolling steadily off the production line in Mesa, Arizona.

The thought-provoking quote that opens this section is correct. Apache with its electronic tools is like nothing else flying today. The cost-effective helicopter described in the pages that follow is not a dream but an extremely capable, real-world machine already flying in significant numbers every day and night. Apache sets a new standard for integrated helicopter design and provides an extremely capable weapons platform on which to build the advances of tomorrow.

First published in 1988 by Motorbooks International
Publishers & Wholesalers, Inc, P.O. Box 2, 729 Prospect Ave. Osceola, WI 54020 USA

© International Defense Images

All rights reserved. With the exception of quoting brief passages for the purposes of review no part of this publication may be reproduced without prior written permission from the publisher.

Motorbooks International is a certified trademark registered with the United States Patent Office

Printed and bound in Japan

The information in this book is true and complete to the best of our knowledge. All recommendations are made without any guarantee on the part of the authors or publisher, who also disclaim any liability incurred in connection with the use of this data or specific details.

Library of Congress Cataloging-in-Publication Data

APACHE MULTI-PURPOSE ATTACK HELICOPTER
A striking analysis in color photography and specification data

1. Apache (Attack Helicopter) I. International Defense Images (Firm)
UG1233.A63 1988   358.4'183--dc19
ISBN 0-87938-303-8

Motorbooks International books are also available at discounts in bulk quantity for industrial or sales-promotional use. For details write to Special Sales Manager at the Publisher's Address.

APACHE
MULTI-PURPOSE ATTACK HELICOPTER

Profile: William P. Brown Page 8	Mission Equipment Page 33	Training/Maintainability Page 70
Overview Page 17	Weapons Page 45	Improvement Program Page 81
Design Details Page 29	Chain Gun Page 65	Deploying Apache Page 86

Written by J. Philip Geddes
Design by David Polewski

EDITORIAL STAFF
Mi Seitelman, Susan Turner, Philip Farris, Gary Kieffer, Susan Mitchell

PHOTOGRAPHY

Frederick Sutter - Front and Back Covers, 1, 4 thru 7, 12, 15, 28 thru 31, 33 thru 45, 48 thru 53, 56 thru 59, 63 (top), 70 (top left), 71, 82-83, 87, 89, 92-93, 96

Mi Seitelman - 18 thru 27, 33, 96

Brian Wolfe - 2-3, 68-69, 74-75

R.W. Ferguson (McDonnell Douglas) - 9 thru 14

Courtesy of McDonnell Douglas Helicopter Company - 16-17, 46-47, 54-55, 62-63, 65, 66-67, 70 bottom, 72-73, 81, 86, 88, 90-91

Courtesy of Rockwell International - 48 (top), 60-61 (top)

Illustration courtesy of General Dynamics - 84-85

Jonathan Scott Arms - Photographic Research

PROFILE: William P. Brown
President, McDonnell Douglas Helicopter Company

Bill Brown is an affable, hands-on manager who became president of McDonnell Douglas Helicopter Company in 1986. Brown is no newcomer to helicopters. He joined McDonnell Douglas Helicopter Company in 1980 as chief engineer, after a 25-year career with the Boeing Company, starting as a stress analyst on the B-52 bomber. In 1964 he began a series of top engineering jobs on Boeing helicopter programs. In this interview with J. Philip Geddes, Mr. Brown paints a broad picture of current events in his company.

The prime driver with respect to our future is meeting the needs of our customers. And that has as much to do with our current products as well as anything we might envision for the future. Reductions in the defense budget present a challenge we must be up to. Industry is increasingly competitive, yet regardless of what competitors are doing, McDonnell Douglas Helicopter Company has a fantastic opportunity. Our customers are emphasizing quality and productivity -- both play a big part in our present and future product lines.

We've had a lot of dialogue with potential civil customers on their needs for future products and as a result are planning a new helicopter for the commercial world. It turns out that civil and military customers alike want helicopters with reasonable cost of ownership, that are easy to maintain, that are very reliable and able to do the job, whether in a utility role such as delivering people or cargo, or putting the right weaponry in the right place at the right time. Economic factors are probably as great, if not greater, for the near term than technical factors. Again, this thinking is paralleled in both military and civil markets. No one wants a Mach 2 helicopter. The whole world is looking toward economy and reliability of operation for helicopters.

PUT A FACE ON YOUR CUSTOMER (sign on cafeteria wall in the Mesa, AZ facility)

We've accepted that instilling customer quality as a state of mind is our biggest challenge this year. Aiming to lower scrap rates and deliver defect-free products are the easiest quality goals to measure. But quality goes beyond that when we recognize that the customer for most people in this company isn't someone on the outside at all, it's someone right here inside. So, in this context, quality means many things that are often overlooked as trivial, going right down to writing memos and letters that do not have typing errors, recognizing that you owe your customer, whoever that customer may be, a quality effort. This kind of quality is a grass roots effort that takes in everyone, not just the shop floor.

MACHINING and CELLS

In the past, a part going through its fabrication cycle, starting at rough machining, may have been sent over to another building for the next step. Now, we're collecting all the machines through which particular parts flow, into a local area or cell. This means that if I'm the fellow who does the rough machining, I turn that part over to someone right next to me. I look him in the eye when delivering my product. He is my customer. I am accountable for the quality of my work. And in that simple case, handing a part to the man who handles the next sequence provides a more personal identification than throwing it in a cart heading for another building, knowing that you will never see it again. Personal contact creates more personal concern for the quality of that part. The old axiom that you don't inspect quality into a product is true. We are really trying to minimize inspection and emphasize personal accountability, everywhere.

In our helicopter divisions we have introduced a concept we call "co-location." As an example, on the Model 500 light helicopter line, instead of grouping engineers in one building and manufacturing planners in another, we co-located all the men and women associated with the product together. I'm convinced that in aerospace, you get greater esprit de corps and performance if the focus is more on the product than on a professional discipline. As a stress engineer, I found a greater sense of satisfaction and pride by identifying with a particular vehicle that was going to fly, rather than presenting a paper on stress analysis. In aerospace, where you are always developing something new, it's easy to focus on a product that puts you right out on the front edge of technology. And we can do that in the commercial world just as well as in the military world or in research and development (R & D).

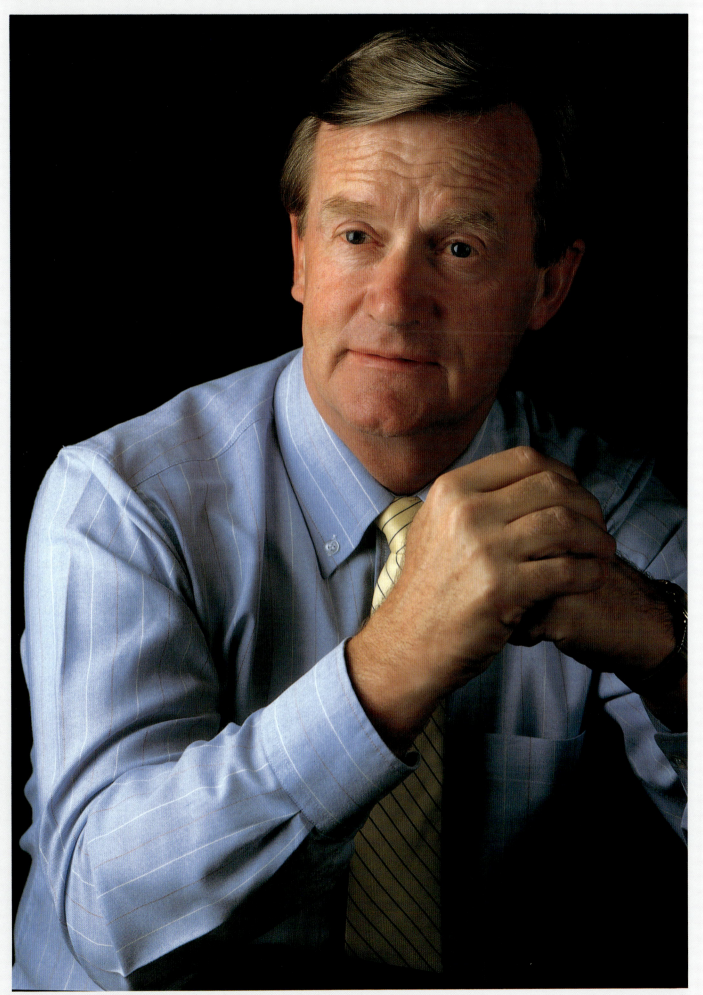

SILO BUSTING

A positive attitude is a primary ingredient for success in quality. Attitude is the catalyst that promotes a sense of teamwork, of pride. When we all operate under the same concept of what we are trying to achieve as a team, we break down communications barriers. At times we refer to our splinter activities as "silos" -- there's the engineering silo, the quality control silo, the manufacturing silo and so on. For about a year and half now, we've been silo busting, which means getting everybody to work together.

Hierarchy isn't important -- teamwork is, which means that a little bit of ego deflation is not out of place. To run the race and give it your best shot is what's important. At the same time I have to care what the competition is doing because we live in a very competitive world where you win or you lose at great expense in terms of investment that does not lead to sales. The U.S. Army's new LHX helicopter project is an example of where our major team members have joined us in big investments. With LHX as a rallying point, focusing on the end product is very good for morale, no matter what the limits of any one person's job may be.

THE WORK FORCE

We have a mix of fairly new and senior employees. In fact we have the best of both worlds -- veteran employees who are both skilled and dedicated, and a younger work force anxious to carve out careers in our business and eager to go to work for a company willing to help fulfill their dreams. Management's task is to continuously expose them all to new and challenging tasks. This dynamic is our trademark. Our work force of about 5,500 in Arizona is younger than in California; about 1,600 actually moved from California and the others were hired here in Arizona. Many came from other parts of the country and relocated to Arizona. We still have a solid, very senior work force of 2,000 in Culver City, which overall, gives us continuity and the benefit of excellent experience, coupled with the younger aggressive work force in Arizona. We're doing all we can to help our employees reach their full potential.

Our company invests 40 hours per person per year in training. That may not seem like much but with 7,500 people that adds up to 300,000 hours overall, a lot for a small company. And that's stepped up almost double from last year. In a major effort to provide career opportunity, company courses are conducted on the premises and continuing education is encouraged at several universities in Arizona and California. Our supervisors in their 40-hour training period look at how to do a better job in interpersonal relations and efficiency in production. Every one of our exempt personnel has finished an eight hour course in ethics, based on the firm belief that ethics is the strong foundation of a successful company.

FACILITIES

In moving to Arizona from California, we had the opportunity to design a facility from the ground up that is efficient for our particular business. Our 340,000-square-foot Advanced Development Center, which houses engineering and the development labs, is the most modern in the helicopter world. This gives us outstanding technical capabilities to compete effectively for new business. We have electronics laboratories, composite structures laboratories, simulators, and all of the support equipment needed to develop new products in the helicopter world. That plus people-oriented office space and a modern production line gives us the tremendous boost of a "total" facility.

OUT OF THE PAST

Many customers who think that our company is technologically superior talk about items such as crashworthiness of the OH-6 which was developed for the Vietnam era. They identify Hughes Helicopters, now McDonnell Douglas Helicopter Company, as providing a superb little machine that had good performance and survivability. Pilots liked the OH-6 for its fine handling qualities and rugged design. But there was a negative side. In the past we were seen as a good, innovative company with a lot of ingenious engineers who came up with good products but, after fielding those products, there was a lack of diligence with respect to follow up.

We cannot be accused of that today. For example, when we introduced the Apache into the field at Fort Hood, Texas, the point of single station fielding for the helicopter, we made being a field service representative a prestigious assignment. We have excellent people with a customer focus in mind, and who are technically competent. They are interested, with our customers, from the outset in digging out all issues that might bear on the successful fielding of the helicopter. Any problem has a direct tie into the factory. I continue to monitor the progress of the Apache in the field and visited Fort Hood four times last year. We do not lose interest in a product once it flies over the fence to a customer and feel very strongly about continued product support.

THE APACHE RECORD

Apache has been very good in the field. First off, it has exceeded Army specifications substantially in terms of power, speed and vertical climb capability. If you talk about maintainability and availability, the Army's standard measures of reliability, it is doing very well. Maintenance man hours on the Apache are a remarkable 4.6 hours per flight hour against a spec permitting 9.0 maintenance hours per flight hour. Availability in terms of average operational readiness is running a couple of points over the spec requirement of 80%. In the REFORGER exercises last fall in Germany two Army Apache battalions had a mission availability of over 85%. They also had a good logistics pipeline to support the aircraft. When a new aircraft goes into the field, spare parts and support can become a problem, which is why 1987 at McDonnell Douglas Helicopter Company was proclaimed "the year of the spare."

In the "year of the spare," all levels of management were made to feel very strongly about meeting delivery commitments for spares. At the start of the year our delinquency rate was 40% and ended up at about 2%. It took a lot of effort at all levels to get those numbers down. The initial problem came when we were trying to build the production line and keep up with a lot of spares orders at the same time. But there are a couple of ways of keeping score on spares deliveries: one is of the number of parts and the other is the way the military does it, with the number of contract line items. For example, if the Army had ordered 15 transmissions and had taken delivery on 14, our score stayed at zero until they got the fifteenth. Our internal method, on the other hand, is tracking the number of parts. But no matter how you keep score, we succeeded.

APACHE AS A WEAPONS PLATFORM

Apache is a very good weapons platform and the users are upbeat. During my visits to Fort Hood I saw first hand how well things went in battalion exercises by flying in the front seat of an Apache going out on simulated combat missions. Flight briefings and debriefings showed convincingly that the Apache is giving the Army a capability well beyond anything they have had to date. This sounds self serving but it's a clear impression of what I heard.

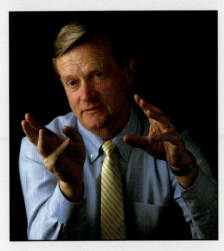

When Lt. General Saint was commander at Fort Hood, he had five Apache battalions under his command; two of these were taken to Europe last fall for REFORGER. In REFORGER he changed his operating tactics to emphasize night operations because he had gained a significant advantage from Apache's ability to fight at night, using operating systems that were vastly superior to what he had before. The Apaches, he told me, were decisive with respect to the outcome of the exercise.

Apache has substantial power margins and is essentially a vibration free aircraft which greatly reduces pilot fatigue. Contemporary helicopters carry a lot of heavy systems to make the pilot feel more comfortable and reduce vibration. We don't carry an ounce of vibration isolation equipment on the Apache. I can't claim that that's the result of superior technology. Nevertheless, the result is very desirable from a pilot's viewpoint and also has a positive effect on parts life. The flight workload is manageable; the copilot gunner in the front seat operates the weapons and the pilot in the back seat handles the flying and the navigation, which provides a sensible split of the workload. Our attack helicopter experience is so good that we have taken a lot of Apache technology to the LHX light helicopter that we are working on jointly with Bell Helicopter and McDonnell Douglas Aircraft Company.

Similarly, a lot of our experience in the simulation area is helping develop systems with reduced pilot workload, so much so that we believe that the LHX can be a one-man machine. LHX as a one-man machine is somewhat controversial at this stage but technologically it is feasible. Experienced pilots who are flying our one-man machine in simulators confirm that a single pilot can do this job.

The Army has found it desirable to bring younger pilots into the Apache program. They don't seem to have the inhibitions acquired on older aircraft which lack the capability of our helicopter. The Apache has even demonstrated loops and rolls. Although flying a helicopter upside down is unconventional, it illustrates the forgiving nature of the Apache.

FUTURE DEVELOPMENT

The evolution of the Apache will be a departure from what was once typical for a helicopter. Apache has proved to be such a solid platform at this stage, that changes being planned are not related to improving performance or refining flying qualities. I see the evolution of the Apache in mission equipment, in terms of the guns, missiles, rockets or new weapons that are coming along, and in terms of advanced avionics that might be used. Our basically modular design, with a digital data bus system, lets you plug in different black boxes and weapons and is adaptable to new components in the mission equipment package. Right now we have the flexibility to carry various types of weapons; for example, we are flight testing an Apache for air-to-air combat, using three contending missiles: the STINGER, SIDEWINDER and MISTRAL. All three are being evaluated for compatibility on the Apache. Inherent flexibility and adaptability to new pieces of equipment give us a system that should

have a long life and also be meaningful to the international customer.

In discussions at McDonnell Douglas corporate headquarters in St. Louis, I like to say that I envision the Apache as the F-4 of the helicopter world. That is something with which they can identify very quickly but I see the same flexibility in systems as the F-4 also in terms of its use on the international scene. A good aircraft, be it helicopter or fixed wing, has a way of evolving and perpetuating itself. I see that as the future of the Apache. So, while we don't have to solve performance and airframe problems at this stage, our company has to do three things: develop the advanced configuration, keep the program sold to the Army, then sell it on the international scene. We have lots of work ahead of us but we don't have to apologize technically for our Apache.

Whether the Apache can do the job for which it was designed is never an issue. Issues may relate to development costs for advanced configurations, to production costs as we diminish production rates to keep it affordable in the overall military scene and things of that nature. We don't set requirements but when you give your customer more than he required by exceeding performance specifications, you have a tremendous advantage in terms of the continuation of a project.

COST OF APACHE

The biggest issue with respect to the Apache has been cost and affordability. Looking back to the 1981 time frame, the Army's acquisition review identified a requirement for 446 aircraft and a unit cost estimate of $13.8 million. We are now delivering Apaches at a million dollars less per machine than was authorized when the program started. Cost hasn't grown. As a matter of fact, this is the only aircraft, in my experience, where the unit cost for the first six production lots, has decreased every year. Not only have we overcome inflation but the unit cost has gone down as well. And we are not talking equivalent 1972 dollars (when the program was launched) or 1980 dollars (when the first AH-64 rolled out) or 1988 dollars: in real dollars the aircraft has gotten cheaper each year.

When you start talking unit cost, first of all you have to establish the ground rules on whether it includes initial spares, ground support equipment, amortization of tooling, paying for a program management office in the Army, recoupment of R&D and so on. There are so many ways to quote unit cost that you have to set your standard for calculation and then the number pops out. Under our company's current fiscal year contract with the Army, the recurring unit cost for hardware alone is $6.87 million. Flyaway and program costs are calculated on an entirely different basis.

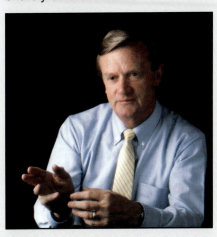

R & D

Our independent R & D efforts were sparked considerably after we were acquired by McDonnell Douglas in January 1984. Prior to that we were operating under very limited budgets. McDonnell Douglas was able to take a long range view on programs like LHX and the elements necessary to be competitive in the helicopter world. In addition, we transplanted the bulk of the company, except our fabrication center, over to Arizona from California. When we came to Arizona we expanded a facility with 570,000 square feet to over two million square feet today. There was a $300 million investment when we made the move, so obviously McDonnell Douglas is not in it for the short haul.

COMMERCIAL OPERATIONS AND MDX

Our civil business is dominated by the fortunes of small operators and that market has been very depressed. The health of the commercial market is still largely driven by the oil companies, for exploration, servicing oil rigs and so forth. There are signs however, of a turnaround. The used helicopter market is much more active than a year ago and very few machines are idle. If operators continue to fly at the current rate, that in itself is going to create a demand for replacement equipment just to continue the job being done today.

Right now we are doing our homework in preliminary design on the new MDX helicopter, trying to determine what the world needs. We want to be ready with the right product at the right time. A new helicopter presents a big risk -- not technically but economically. From the start we are discussing participation in MDX with other companies. If we embark on this new development it will be with a partner, either domestic or international, to generate the resources and market needed for the project.

There are a lot of offshoots of our research work in technology and military work that will substantially reduce the operating costs of the new helicopter. All the operators we have surveyed say they want to see us come out with this new machine. But they don't have to buy; they can either accept it or reject it. We've been waiting for the user community to show the sense of need that is now on the rise. That means we are preparing for the next step. In the meantime we will maintain the Model 500 production rate at 72 aircraft a year as we did last year. This way we always have a backlog for the Model 500 without building a large inventory. It's true that the Model 500 rate is obviously well below the several hundred a year that we were building back in the 1980-81 time frame; on the other, hand we are well down the production curve so we can build them relatively efficiently. It is our intention to continue the 500 and make product improvements with updated engines, and bigger rotors. A NOTAR (TM) no-tail-rotor system will be installed on a preproduction aircraft next year and we will get FAA certification in 1990. Beginning roughly in the 1990 time frame, our commercial helicopters could be delivered with NOTAR.

GUNS

Not many people know that we are the country's largest producer of medium-sized automatic cannons, using the Chain Gun (R) concept. We are building the 25mm Bushmaster for the Bradley Fighting Vehicle and the Marine Light Armored Vehicle at about 60 a month in the second year of a five-year multi-year contract. So far we've delivered approximately 4,700 25mm cannons. Then there is the 30mm for the Apache and the 7.62mm produced under license by Royal Ordnance in the U.K. A number of 25mm M242s have been sold to the U.S. Navy for deck mounting on small ships; in fact, many are already at sea including service in the Persian Gulf.

We have proved that Chain Gun (R) cannons, with external motors for constant feed velocity, have very good reliability compared with conventional gas-powered guns. The measure of reliability in a gun is expressed in mean rounds between failures; with the M242 requirement at 6,000 rounds, the actual weapons in service demonstrate more than 20,000 rounds before failure. Our success can be seen in the competition for the Forward Area Air Defense System, won by Martin Marietta, in which the Army directed that all four competitors use the Bushmaster as their gun weapon.

We are very active in gun research with Ordnance taking a proportional share of our R&D budget. Another 30mm weapon, which we call the ASP 30, for Automatic Self Powered, is being tested by the U.S. Army. ASP 30 is intended for a number of land vehicles, such as retrofit on the M113 armored personnel carrier which is used around the world. We are also working on a growth version of Bushmaster for land vehicles. This design differs from the current 25mm cannon for the Bradley by using a longer barrel and larger round to achieve a much higher lethality.

Capability for designing, building and integrating gun systems is highly desirable when you are producing military helicopters. McDonnell Douglas Helicopter Company is also in competition for a small infantry weapon, the AIWS (Advanced Infantry Weapon System), which is to replace the M-16. We won a development contract, one of five, under which we are working on new designs and testing new concepts, including ammunition.

INTERNATIONAL ACTIVITIES

Given that development costs for new aircraft are considerable and requirements for helicopters in many countries are very similar to what the Army has developed in its latest attack helicopter, several countries are very interested in the Apache. I am confident we will have sold Apaches to at least one and perhaps as many as three countries by the end of 1989.

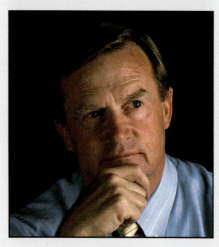

There is a strong sentiment in Europe to buy European. This can be an inordinately expensive and time-consuming approach. Using the numbers I see published, where the Germans require 212 aircraft and the French require 215, the cost is quoted as $8.54 billion. This includes development, qualification and production. That comes out to $20 million per aircraft. The Apache can satisfy Franco German requirements today -- because the threat exists today -- and also because it is more affordable.

Yet we understand that the European antiarmor helicopter program reflects a sense of national purpose by the countries involved. They wish to maintain their domestic development capability and thus look at the program as an investment rather than a purchase.

However, buying U.S. in this case would be cost-effective. Not only that, this approach avoids technical risk. McDonnell Douglas Helicopter Company conducted an extensive development program on the Apache because there generally are numerous fits and starts in the development of any advanced aircraft system. You learn through experience and, as a matter of fact, some of our experience was frustrating. And it takes time to develop a sophisticated system.

We believe our allies can achieve both domestic and defense objectives through participation in the Apache program. We realize we must offer incentives for participation by industries in potential AH-64 customer countries, providing both technological participation and skilled jobs. Options include building aircraft under license, and offsetting purchase price with industrial participation or countertrade. Whatever the formula, we look forward to a successful international phase of the Apache program and anticipate it will begin shortly.

We are a dynamic billion-dollar company active on many fronts, and a significant force in the helicopter and ordnance businesses. Our physical resources, particularly our new headquarters facility, are second to none and will enable us to maintain the lead in technology and production efficiency. We have established a firm base for the future with outstanding professionals and our partnerships with many of the world's leading high technology companies. We also offer the strength of associate companies in the McDonnell Douglas organization. Quality and customer service will remain our guiding lights, and will be embodied in every Apache helicopter we deliver.

Apache's sophisticated mission equipment package has advanced nap-of-the-earth fighting to a fine art. Terrain masking, standoff strike range, and electronic countermeasures with a heavy load of weapons ensure that the Apache remains a powerful strike force at any time and in any weather.

APACHE HAS BEEN DESIGNED FOR COMBAT SURVIVABILITY AND CRASHWORTHINESS.

Load-Absorbing Collapsible Landing Gear

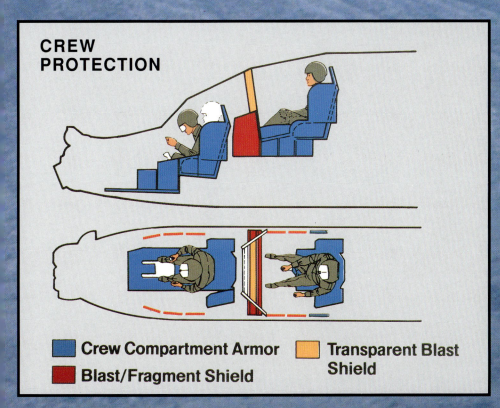

CREW PROTECTION

- Crew Compartment Armor
- Blast/Fragment Shield
- Transparent Blast Shield

Design for survivability, more visible in the crew compartments than elsewhere, is a fundamental part of the overall Apache. In earlier helicopters, protection for the crew or sensitive systems was for the most part a matter of adding armored shields of one kind or another. In Apache, as will be noted in more detail, every system and subsystem, every component, has been designed with an eye to keeping the aircraft flying and fighting in the face of heavy fire. In some cases redundancy and separation promote ballistic tolerance; in others, shielding is appropriate. Excellent performance with impressive firepower is another unmistakable facet of fighting and surviving and when all else fails, so is crashworthiness. All of these elements are basic to the Apache design.

FROM THEORY TO REALITY

Apache was not conceived in a vacuum. Military planners in the West have seen the armored strength of the Warsaw Pact armies increase annually since the early days of the cold war until the current imbalance was realized. Not only have opposing tanks and their weapons become more powerful, they are fielded in a phalanx of support armor including high rate of fire mobile antiaircraft batteries. The U.S. Army, recognizing that rapidly deployable attack helicopters were a logical counter to a first strike tank force, began a series of design and development programs looking for a rotary-winged solution.

In 1972, after several false starts largely aborted by changing analysis of the threat, six companies competed for an ambitious, new state-of-the-art advancement to be called the Advanced Attack Helicopter. The six entrants were then down-selected to two with McDonnell Douglas Helicopter Company (then Hughes Helicopters) and Bell Helicopter awarded contracts for Phase I development. Bell had entered its Model 409, a derivative of the Sea Cobra later designated by the Army as the YAH-63 (the Y stands for prototype) and Hughes Helicopters entered the Model 77, officially designated the YAH-64. The dual winners continued in head-to-head competition building two flying prototypes plus separate ground and static test vehicles. Practical flight demonstrations of the prototypes peaked in the Summer of 1976 as the Army subjected both designs to a final demanding flyoff to pick the winner.

The go-ahead to McDonnell Douglas for Phase II Apache came in December 1976, when full-scale engineering development began. In the long, final development phase, the concept proven by flight testing prototypes was carried into detailed design and tooling made to mass produce the machine. First production was authorized in 1982, only after the emerging helicopter satisfied the customer, the Department of Defense and the Congress, that Apache could fulfill its appointed mission and achieve a service life of 4,500 hours. In the course of development from 1973 to the first production delivery in January 1984, the Apache prototypes flew over 4,000 hours, launched 72 HELL-FIRE missiles and 4,200 folding fin rockets. In addition, Apaches fired 41,000 rounds from the 30mm M230 cannon, designed and built by McDonnell Douglas Helicopter Company.

(Above) The YAH-64 prototype undergoes extensive testing in the desert of the Southwest. (Right) A skilled test pilot probes the edge of the envelope during flight testing.

The Army specification for the new advanced attack helicopter called for the AH-64A to carry eight anti-tank missiles, 320 rounds of 30mm ammunition, sufficient fuel for a 1.83 hour mission and still achieve a vertical rate of climb of at least 450 feet per minute on an Army standard hot day of 95° F at 4,000 feet altitude. The Apache that emerged from its rigorous development and test schedule exceeded the climb requirement, achieving a remarkable 1,450 feet per minute at full power.

A thumbnail sketch of production Apache's performance on a standard day reveals: a cruise speed of 154 knots true air speed (285 kph) at sea level, and at the primary mission gross weight of 14,779 lb. (6718 kg) a hover out-of-ground effect at 11,500 feet (3505 m); a hover in-ground effect at 15,000 feet (4572 m) and a vertical rate of climb of 2,460 feet per minute (750m per minute). Flight sideways and rearward is possible at 45 knots (83 kph). The maneuverability envelope from plus 3.5g to minus 0.5g means that the aircraft is capable of performing very rapid changes in flight path when flying close to the ground or in air-to-air combat without overloading the structure. Design mission endurance of 2.67 hours at sea level gives the helicopter ample provision to get to a distant engagement and loiter at the scene. Low vibration in the cockpit means that the two-man crew can fly extended missions without the bone-rattling fatigue prevalent in older design military helicopters.

Apache may be an ugly duckling but in flight, armed to the teeth, it is a remarkable machine with long legs, capable of carrying ordnance totaling over 6,500 pounds (2948 kg), a feat unsurpassed by any of its predecessors. For a 1,000-nautical mile (1829 km) ferry mission, the gross weight can be increased to 21,000 pounds (9525 kg) with auxiliary fuel. Details of the airframe systems and how the electronics are integrated follow.

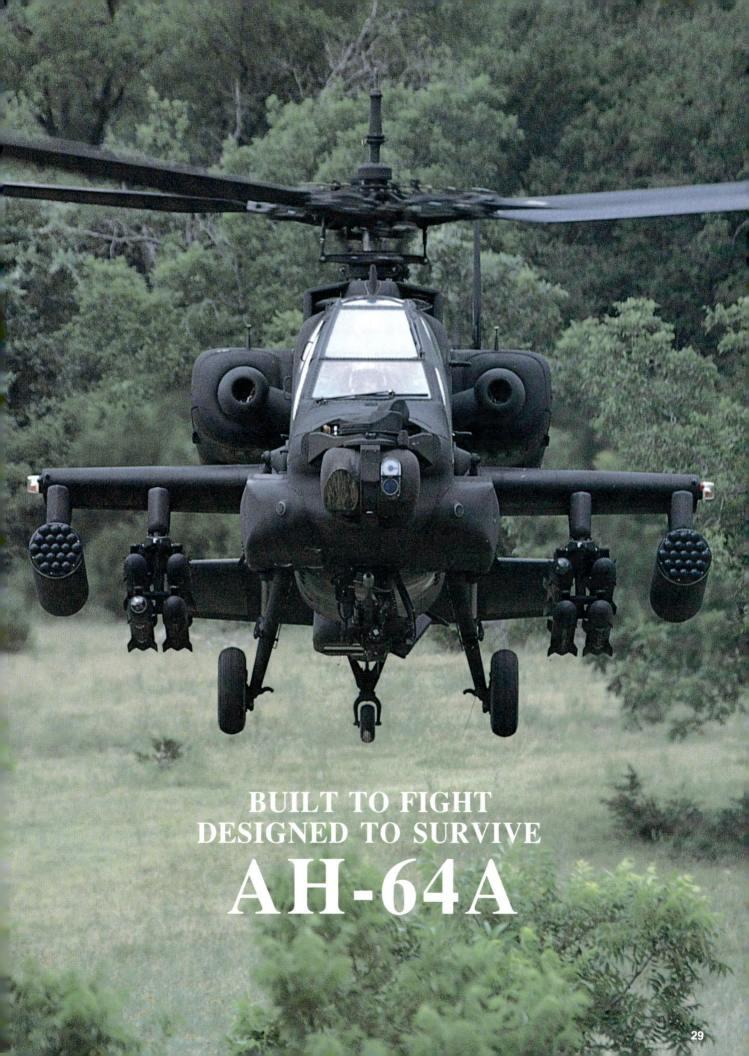

BUILT TO FIGHT DESIGNED TO SURVIVE
AH-64A

Airframe. Flight loads, crashworthiness and landing loads are noted by the designers as the foremost considerations in designing the fuselage. The aircraft is designed to be invulnerable to single impacts of 12.7mm armor-piercing incendiary rounds. Individual components will survive a hit by a single 23mm high explosive, incendiary projectile. After most hits the Apache should be able to complete its mission and return to base by continuing to fly for 30 minutes.

This high ballistic tolerance comes from a set of design criteria used throughout the airframe and all systems that include: redundancy and separation, isolation of sensitive components, damage-resistant forgings and machined components, suppressing system fluid leakage, fire-resistant subsystems, materials that do not shatter on impact, masking and armor plating. Armor is last on this list because it is a dead weight that contributes nothing to agility and overall flight performance and eats into payload. Most of the armor on Apache (99%) is used for crew and fuel protection. Crew seats and protective panels are made of lightweight boron carbide bonded to Kevlar backing. As another example of anticipating worst-case ballistic hits, a high strength steel armor panel between the hydraulic heat exchangers can stop a 12.7mm API projectile penetrating both units.

Redundant semi-monocoque construction, with aluminum alloy longerons, frames and skins, is used throughout the airframe structure. The forward fuselage is designed to

absorb the energy of a crash in which the crew will walk away after the nose slams head-on into an obstruction at 20 feet per second. The forward structure is also made to withstand impact with minimum damage to the crew compartment should the helicopter hit with the nose angled 15 degrees down while moving at 60 feet per second. Fuselage design insures that the crew would survive a vertical impact of 42 feet per second.

The high-visibility canopy is strong enough to withstand the impact of a rotor blade hit and also protect the crew from being crushed in a rollover crash. Pilot and copilot enter their positions through canopy doors on the right side. Canopy side panels can be jettisoned in an emergency by either crew member or a rescue team. Use of contoured glass panels in the canopy reduces glint, a major visual aid to an enemy trying to detect an aircraft.

The trailing landing gear is fixed and consists of two main wheels and a free-swivelling, lockable tail wheel. This gear is capable of protecting the fuselage in a 12 feet per second vertical impact with the nose up 15 degrees and the cockpit tilted 12 degrees to the side. Under these conditions, the aircraft would survive and remain flight worthy except for damage to the gear itself and the rotor striking the ground. Landings and takeoffs are possible at full gross weight on sloping terrain that tilts the nose up or down 12 degrees. Apache can also land, with no wind, on a slope that tilts ten degrees sideways.

NOTABLE PROGRAM MILESTONES FOR APACHE

Dec	1976	McDonnell Douglas Helicopter Company (then Hughes Helicopters, Inc) receives a contract for full scale development of the YAH-64 Advanced Attack Helicopter.
Dec	1976	Company receives first Army contract to produce the 30mm M230 automatic cannon for the Apache. The M230 is based on the company's successful Chain Gun ® concept.
Nov	1982	Company receives the first contract for production of the Apache.
Feb	1983	Apache prototypes log 4,000 combined flight hours.
Apr	1983	Fiscal Year 1983 production contracts totaling $549 million for procurement of 48 Apaches are awarded; 59 aircraft now approved for production.
Jul	1983	Apache assembly and flight test center in Mesa, Arizona completed on schedule 16 months after ground breaking. The plant is the most advanced helicopter assembly facility in the world.
Aug	1983	Congress authorizes production of 112 AH-64s for FY 84.
Sep	1983	First production Apache rolls out two months ahead of schedule.
Jan	1984	Army accepts first production AH-64A one month ahead of contract schedule.
Feb	1984	Army signs $848.1 million contract for third year of Apache production covering 112 AH-64s. Total of 171 AH-64s now funded for production.
Jul	1984	Production and prototype Apaches reach 5,000 total flight hours. With ground tests, Apaches have an overall operation time of more than 8,000 hours.
Aug	1984	AH-64A Apache Production Vehicle No. 2 fires first production HELLFIRE laser-guided missiles during testing at Yuma, Arizona.
Aug	1984	Secretary of Defense approves an AH-64A procurement increase of 160 aircraft -- from 515 to 675 Apaches.
Jan	1985	First production AH-64A Apache to be delivered to an Army base arrives at U.S. Army Aviation Training Center, Ft. Rucker, Alabama.
Jun	1985	U.S. Army, Air Force personnel prepare and load six AH-64A Apaches into a C-5A transport aircraft in less than six hours to certify loading procedures for air deployment of the attack helicopter.
Feb	1986	Production Apaches pass 10,000 flight hours, bringing total production and prototype flight time to more than 15,000 hours.
Mar	1986	McDonnell Douglas Helicopter Company's 100th AH-64A Apache attack helicopter for the U.S. Army rolls off the assembly line at the company's Mesa, Arizona assembly, flight test and delivery center.
Oct	1986	Apache 171 rolls off Mesa, Arizona assembly line, completing third fiscal year (FY 84) products contract for 112 helicopters.
Nov	1986	Delivery of production vehicle 171 to the Army completes fiscal year 1984 contract, which called for production of 112 AH-64s.
Dec	1986	Apache helicopter fleet surpasses 30,000 production flight hours. Trained Army Apache aviators total 270.
Feb	1987	McDonnell Douglas Helicopter Company delivers the 200th AH-64 attack helicopter to the U.S. Army one month ahead of contract schedule.
Apr	1987	AH-64A Apache participates for the first time in the U. S. Army's Air-to-Air Combat Test (AACT) exercises at the Patuxent River Naval Air Test Center, Maryland.
May	1987	McDonnell Douglas AH-64A attack helicopter fleet records 50,000th production flight hour.
May	1987	First government funding for the Advanced Apache program is authorized by congressional committees.
Jun	1987	AH-64A from the U.S. Army Aviation Center at Fort Rucker, Alabama becomes first production Apache to log 1,000 flying hours.
Sep	1987	AH-64A Apache participates for the first time in NATO's REFORGER (Return of Forces to Germany) exercises.
Oct	1987	McDonnell Douglas, under contract to the U.S. Army, launches program to integrate STINGER air-to-air missile into AH-64A Apache weapons systems.
Nov	1987	First test firing of an air-to-air missile from Apache with two AIM-9 SIDEWINDERs launched over White Sands Missile Range, New Mexico.
Dec	1987	300th Apache produced.
Jan	1988	First Apache squadron to be based overseas goes to Illesheim, Germany. Formed and trained at Fort Hood, the 2nd Squadron, 6th Cavalry became the first of 14 battalions planned for permanent basing in Europe between this date and 1992.
Feb	1988	First live firing of a HELLFIRE antiarmor missile by an operational AH-64A attack helicopter unit, at the Army's Yuma, Arizona range.
Apr	1988	Direct hit scored on target with first SIDEARM antiradiation missile firing from an AH-64A.
May	1988	Apache fleet flight time (excluding development flight hours) passes 100,000 hours.
Jun	1988	Charles Parlier and Edward Wilson presented with the Fredrick L. Feinberg Award for flying the Apache in air-to-air combat development tests.
Jun	1988	McDonnell Douglas Helicopter Company and Army Aviation Technology Directorate (Intelligent Fault Locator Team) selected to receive the Harry T. Jensen Award for leadership in developing technologies improving the readiness and support of the U.S. Army Helicopters Combined Arms team.

APACHE POWER
MUSCLE IN MOTION

Powerplants. Apache is powered by two General Electric T700-GE-701 turboshaft engines rated at 1,694 shaft horsepower each, driving the main rotor through engine nose-mounted gearboxes connected to the main transmission. Either of these exceptionally reliable turbine engines can offset a single failure by the remaining engine providing the pilots with a maximum power output of 1,728 shaft horsepower. The single engine service ceiling at mission gross weight on a standard day is 10,800 feet.

Auxiliary ground power for engine starting, electrical, pressurized air and hydraulic power is supplied by a single auxiliary power unit connected to the main transmission accessory drive section. On-board auxiliary power makes the Apache independent of external starting systems and provides electrical power for systems tests while on the ground.

The engines are mounted, widely-separated, on each side of the fuselage structure on a fail- safe mounting system using three primary mounts backed by two normally unloaded secondary mounts. Should the primary support system fail, the secondary mounts can carry the engines.

Hot gases streaming from turbine engines create hot exhaust structures making a natural target for enemy infrared (IR) guided missiles. On Apache, the engines are safety wrapped by means of a Black Hole Ocarina (BHO) infrared suppression system. Cold external air is drawn in from an external vent, circulated around the engine then mixed with the turbine exhaust. The Black Hole system lowers the temperature of the exhaust gases and hot engine structure to the point where they are no longer detectable. This simple system has no moving parts.

Hydraulic, Pneumatic and Electrical Systems. All flight controls, except the electrically operated stabilator trim on the tail, are driven by the dual hydraulic system. Hydraulics also power the external stores pylons, the chin turret for the 30mm M230 cannon and the rotor brake. The hydraulic system also starts the auxiliary power unit and unlocks the tail wheel. The primary hydraulic system is used exclusively for the flight control system; all other hydraulic functions are part of a secondary or utility subsystem. Should any hydraulically powered auxiliary component be damaged, the flight control part of the system is automatically isolated. Flight controls are further backed up by an electro-hydraulic "fly-by-wire" control system in case any primary mechanical controls are severed or jam. Flight control hydraulic actuators and yaw actuators are made of high-strength steel to increase ballistic tolerance.

Pressurized air is used to operate the environmental control system, engine starters, fuel boost pump, fuel transfer pump, engine firewall cooling louvers and pressurizing reservoirs. The environmental control system supplies air conditioning and heating for both crew members, the avionic black boxes and the TADS/PNVS turret in the nose. Toxic gases and fumes are kept out of the crew area by cabin pressurization and venting.

AC power at 115/200 volt, three-phase, 400 Hz is distributed by a four wire system. Power is generated by two 35 KVA alternators mounted on the main transmission accessory gearbox; either alternator can supply the full electrical load. DC power is supplied by two 250 ampere transformer rectifiers. Emergency electrical backup comes from a 24 volt nickel cadmium battery which, when 90% charged, can supply the emergency electrical load for 12 minutes following the loss of all normal electrical power. Ground power can be supplied by either the on-board auxiliary power unit or through an external ground power receptacle.

Fuel System. Apache's fuel is stored in two separate main fuel cells, one with 156 gallon (590 liter) usable capacity located forward of the ammunition bay and the second of 220 gallon (833 liter) aft of the ammunition bay. There is provision on the stub wings for four 230 gallon (870 liter) pylon mounted auxiliary tanks that extend range to 1,000 nautical miles.

In all operations, positive nitrogen pressure is maintained in the fuel tanks. This lays an inert gas blanket over the fuel to prevent a fire should a tank be pierced by an incendiary round. The cells self seal by means of foam and backing board that closes around the hole blasted by a 12.7mm round rupturing the tank. Should 14.5mm armor-piercing incendiaries hit the cells, they will seal sufficiently to retain a 30 minute fuel supply.

Apache can be refueled and rearmed in ten minutes, even when operating in the forward area near a battle, using pressure or gravity fill ports. Rapid refueling is possible through a single-point system in four minutes.

Rotor System. Apache is lifted on a four-bladed fully articulated main rotor system. The blade retention straps flex to allow blade flapping and feathering movements. Flapping hinges are offset and the lead-lag hinge is restricted by redundant elastomeric dampers. A hydraulic rotor brake stops the system turning after flight shutdown. The main rotor blades are removed for ease of transport aboard the C-5A and the future C-17.

The main rotor blades feature four stainless steel spars, which form four structural boxes, reinforced with internal unidirectional fiberglass tubes. Erosion by blowing sand and debris near the ground is reduced by using a heavy-gauge, stainless steel leading edge that makes an effective chopper in bushes and trees. Four-spar design of the airfoil makes it possible to keep flying after absorbing a direct hit from 12.7mm or 23mm high explosive incendiary projectiles. Proof of this was demonstrated by a main rotor blade in simulated flight operating for over five hours after a worst case hit by a 23mm HEI round. This was ten times the requirement.

The blade retention straps on the main rotor hub are of laminated construction with 22 layers to provide inherent flexibility and high strength with excellent damage tolerance. This is demonstrated by the aircraft continuing to fly with 11 of the 22 laminations fractured. The upper and lower blade root fitting and lead-lag links are made strong enough for any one blade attachment lug or mating folding link pair to fail completely in flight without the blade failing. Should either of the dual lead-lag dampers made of elastomeric materials fail after a hit, the remaining damper is strong enough to keep the Apache flying.

The tail rotor consists of two sets of two-bladed teetering hubs mounted in a torsionally flexible fork; setting the blades 55 degrees apart has greatly reduced noise output. Laminated blade retention straps, similar in concept to those on the main rotor hub, are naturally damage tolerant. The titanium hubs mask the root end of the blades from projectiles. The tail rotor is protected from damage during excessive tail-down landings by its high position above the tail boom and stabilator.

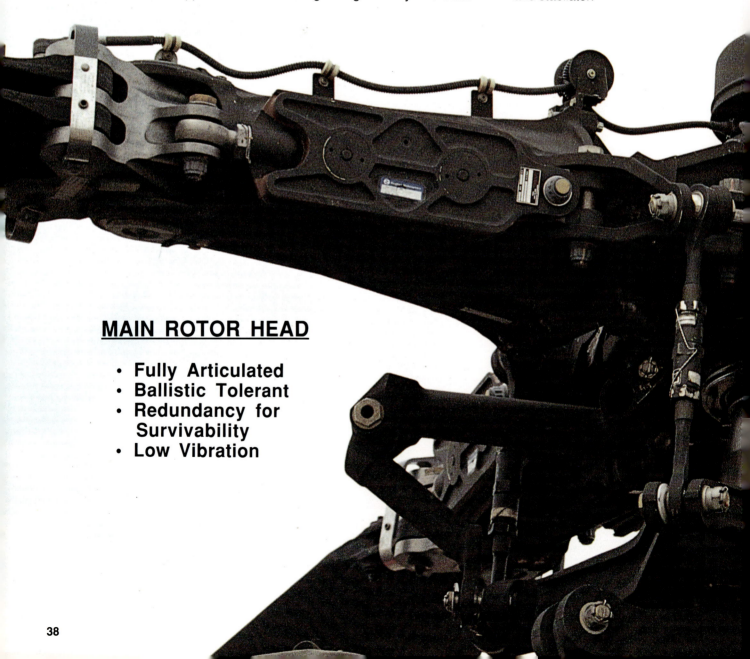

MAIN ROTOR HEAD

- **Fully Articulated**
- **Ballistic Tolerant**
- **Redundancy for Survivability**
- **Low Vibration**

Drive System. Each engine drives the main transmission through a right-angled nose gearbox. The main transmission drives the main rotor shaft and the tail rotor. Two independent oil feed systems keep the transmission lubricated in normal operation. Turbine engine speed is first reduced in the nose gearbox and again in the main transmission by means of a three-stage primary reduction gear system for the main rotor. The main rotor can be braked with engines at ground idle power in winds up to 45 knots (83 km/h) by means of a rotor brake mounted on the transmission. This brake can stop the rotor within 60 seconds from 100% rotor rpm. Should the main transmission fail for any reason in flight, the main rotor drive shaft, which drives through a static mast that carries structural loads, has a shear section to allow Apache to autorotate in an emergency landing. For maintenance, the transmission can be removed without removing the main rotor assembly and the rotor drive shaft can be removed through the rotor hub without disturbing the transmission or removing the hub.

Tail rotor drive shafts transmit power from the main transmission to the tail rotor through a gearbox in the lower vertical tail section of the fuselage and a tail rotor gearbox adjacent to the tail rotor static mast. Tail rotor shafts are located on top of the tail boom and on the forward spar of the vertical stabilizer and are covered by removable fairings for easy access.

Highly stressed transmission and drive components on an ordinary helicopter are likely to fail rapidly once oil supply is lost. On Apache, all drive systems are designed to function for at least 30 minutes with the oil system out of action. In depleted oil supply tests, Apache main transmission and engine nose gearboxes have run for a full hour without lubrication. The gearboxes through which the tail rotor is driven operated for 2 1/2 hours after sustaining multiple ballistic hits. Built-in redundancy in the support trusses reduces the danger of the transmission breaking loose and hurtling into the crew compartment. All critical load bearings in the drive system used steel liners for protection against 12.7mm armor-piercing incendiary rounds. The four-inch diameter (11.43cm) aluminum tail rotor drive shaft can tolerate a hit from a tumbling 12.7mm API round.

FUTURE SKIES FIND APACHE READY

All battlefields are noisy and confusing. Visibility is uncertain, communication difficult. Among the likely scenarios are swiftly moving armored engagements spread over large areas, difficult communications, electronic noise as enemy and defender alike jam the airwaves, long-range strike weapons discharging payloads from nowhere, air-to-ground strikes creating havoc. Ever-changing weather, no matter what the season, can be relied on to lower visibility without much warning and increase the difficulties on the ground.

The typical scenario described above is where Apache has to communicate, navigate, see in reduced visibility, fly hugging the ground, hover behind sheltering cover, find targets and launch weapons against them and live to fight again. The integrated mission equipment package makes it possible for Apache to function well under such adverse battlefield conditions. Both pilot and copilot/gunner, operating as a team, can quickly and accurately transition from en route navigation to acquire targets, then rapidly select and fire their most effective weapons with a high probability of success.

Apache's effectiveness is based on several factors: the aircraft's readiness to take off from a forward area and engage an enemy; ability to navigate accurately from point-to-point; hold exposure time to a minimum during target acquisition and delivery; exhibit a low signature to the enemy when exposed and kill that enemy with the first round, then turn to the next target. The systems in the mission equipment package that make it possible for Apache to perform those functions are as follows:

- Target Acquisition Designation Sight/Pilot Night Vision Sensor (TADS/PNVS)
- Fire Control Computer (FCC)
- Multiplex Data Bus System
- Symbol Generator
- Integrated Helmet and Display Sighting System (IHADSS)
- Heading and Attitude Reference System (HARS)
- Doppler Inertial Navigation Unit
- Air Data System
- HELLFIRE Modular Missile System
- 70mm Folding Fin Aerial Rocket System
- 30mm M230 Automatic Cannon

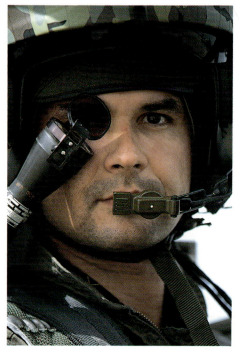

Integrated Displays. The Target Acquisition Designation Sight/Pilot Night Vision Sensor (TADS/PNVS) in the nose turret and the Integrated Helmet and Display Sighting System (IHADSS) are the keys to providing both crew members with sufficient visual cues to make Apache an adverse weather, day and night fighter. During a typical attack mission as Apache enters a target area, the copilot/gunner's optical relay tube on the TADS is used as the primary display. With one switch movement he can select either direct view optics (DVO), day television (DTV), or forward looking infrared (FLIR), depending on visibility.

TADS DVO shows a direct daytime scene through a dual-magnification telescope capable of

greatly increasing an image. TADS DTV provides dual-magnification of daytime scenes, using television imagery to portray the view. DTV, which operates in the upper visual and near infrared region of the spectrum, is powerful enough, even when visibility is poor, to read through camouflage and display targets at very long ranges. In addition to being viewed on the copilot/gunner's optical relay tube, DTV can also be displayed on either crew member's helmet sights. TADS FLIR provides thermal imagery for periods of darkness or reduced visibility during the day and is displayed on both helmet sights. FLIR is the key to penetrating smoke and fog and, because it has a wide field of view, complements the Pilot Night Vision System.

In a typical combat scenario, the pilot scans the target area by looking out of the cockpit. Normal vision for both crew members is augmented by TADS DTV or FLIR displays on their helmet sights. Meanwhile, the copilot/gunner uses the TADS narrow field of view modes to detect and identify targets while the Apache is still at a safe, standoff range. With a field of regard of 120 degrees swivelling in azimuth and 30 degrees up and 60 degrees down, TADS is well suited to fast moving close-in combat situations. Either crew member can direct the other's attention to a potential target by using line-of-sight cueing symbols in the other's display. This greatly cuts the time and difficulty to describe the location of a target.

The Pilot Night Vision Sensor assists in target detection and navigation by using its FLIR sensor, a device that is far more sensitive than the human eye during the day or even night vision helped by special goggles. While the primary function of the PNVS is to free the pilot from the handicap of flying blind at night, the outline of hills, forests, buildings and other features of any landscape are clearly visible around the clock, even with smoke, dust, haze, fog, clouds, snow or sleet.

Target location is normally described in a set of coordinates, degrees of latitude and longitude, or waypoints en route to the target. Fixes are inserted into the fire control computer through a data entry keyboard. The pilot flies to the target coordinates, even though that location may be obscured by the battle or weather, using the Doppler navigation system working with the Heading Attitude Reference system. Steering information from the Doppler Navigator can be displayed on both the pilot and copilot/gunner's helmet mounted displays, while simultaneously directing the Target Acquisition and Designation Sight to target.

En route to a target, such as a group of tanks protected by heavy, mobile antiaircraft pieces, Apache takes advantage of the terrain to stay screened from the enemy. Once within range the helicopter can duck down behind a hill or other natural cover and stay hidden until it's time to attack. Only when the helicopter bobs up to launch a weapon is it exposed to the enemy. Should the crew choose to hold their fire during bob-up from a very limited screened area such as a clearing in dense woods, the pilot can rely on a "return to mask" steering display to fly back into his original cover. He can then repeat the bob-up maneuver whenever he wants.

Any laser-ranging, bearing and elevation fix relative to the aircraft's position taken during a sighting is stored in the fire control computer. The helicopter is free to move around in altitude, range and bearing relative to the target with new fire control information for direct or indirect fire continuously computed. At the right moment, the crew can open fire without having to perform another search and acquisition maneuver. Similarly, while in full defilade, Apache can fire a HELLFIRE missile through a computer developed acquisition window, using a remote laser designator. A remote ground observer, in line-of-sight to the target, can guide a HELLFIRE missile to its target by simply aiming his coded laser designator on the target. Designation can also be provided by another helicopter.

Combat effectiveness is also helped by several other factors such as rapid laser ranging the distance from the target, the short time required to bring lethal suppressive fire to bear, and the weapon system's ability to acquire and track the target no matter what the visibility, day or night. HELLFIRE is capable of stopping all known armor threats.

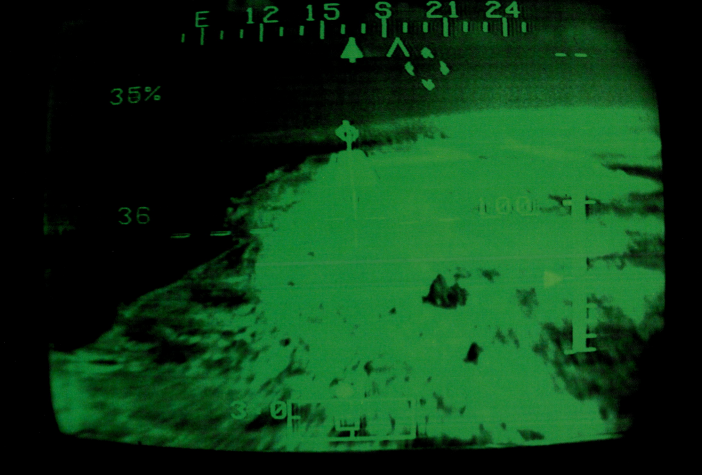

PNVS – PILOT NIGHT VISION SENSOR

The Integrated Helmet and Display Sighting System (IHADSS) presents crew members with a television-type display on a small combining lens. This one square-inch monocle can be read easily with one eye. Flight information needed to maintain safe combat flying status is projected onto the display. For nap-of-the-earth missions in total darkness, the symbology from the flight display is superimposed on a FLIR for true, head-up flight control. When the pilot turns his head, the PNVS turret, which is slaved to the pilot's line-of-sight, turns with him making it second nature to see in the dark. If the gunner in the front seat is occupied elsewhere, the pilot can back up his crew member by directing the gun and delivering suppressive gunfire through his IHADSS. He simply looks at his intended target, places the aim-point symbol on his helmet display on the target and opens fire. PNVS FLIR has been tested over a wide range of climatic conditions including hot, dry, sandy deserts; humid, snow-covered mountains; and hot, humid, heavily forested swamps. Apache's owl-like eyes will work anywhere in the world.

PNVS makes it possible to fight at night using the terrain masking techniques essential to survival during the day. Apache pilots have proven their ability to fly at night in confined areas and hover out-of-ground effect with greater precision than possible with night vision goggles. The IHADSS also makes it possible to determine ranges and closing rates accurately at night, with flight information symbology superimposed on either television or FLIR imagery. No matter where the crew heads turn, the symbology remains in front of their eyes.

Displays can be selected to show flight status symbol-sets, to accommodate different flight modes such as cruise, transition, bob-up and hover. As an example, when he selects the symbol-set for bob-up, the pilot sees all of the normal flight information such as heading, airspeed, altitude, rate of climb and so on, plus the unique symbols for helping the Apache position itself and fire. Two key symbols for bob-up, the "hover box" and "velocity vector," provide control cues for the pilot to fly back to a safe masking spot from which he emerged to fire or take a sight on an enemy.

**APACHE'S WEAPONS
From Acquisition to Weapon Delivery.** The Target Acquisition Designation Sight (TADS) works with the Fire Control Computer (FCC), the Integrated Helmet and Display Sighting System (IHADSS) and the Symbol Generator in the mission equipment package to acquire (select and lock-on) a target. After lock-on, the crew can attack with HELLFIRE missiles, the 30mm M230 cannon, or 70mm rockets. The four ways for the crew to acquire targets are:

• External cue -- TADS or IHADSS line of sight to a ground target. TADS is copilot/gunner operated, IHADSS is operated by both crew members.

• Laser hand-off -- the on-board laser tracker detects laser energy emanating from another helicopter or ground observer. The illuminated target is automatically centered on the Apache's day television, direct view optics or FLIR sensors; both crew members can participate.

• Target of opportunity -- the copilot/gunner selects either the day television, direct view optics or FLIR sensors, then steers the TADS by line-of-sight in the manual mode using a thumb control.

• Pre-programmed targets -- target locations are entered into the FCC. When the Apache is unmasked the TADS is pre-pointed, looking at the target location to reduce exposure.

HELLFIRE MISSILES

70mm ROCKETS

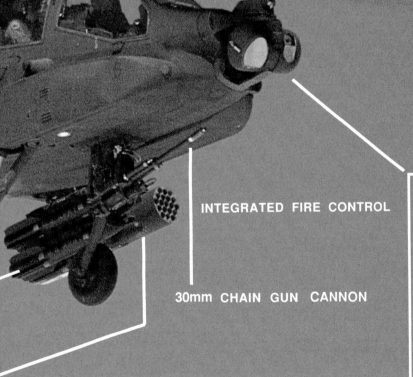

PILOT NIGHT VISION SENSOR (PNVS)

- Stabilized Forward Looking Infrared (FLIR)
- Azimuth ± 90°
- Elevation +20° to -45°
- Slue Rate 120°/sec
- Fields of View (One)
  - - Wide
    - 50° Diagonal
    - 1 Power
    - Far Visual Range 8-14 Microns

INTEGRATED HELMET AND DISPLAY SIGHTING SYSTEM

INTEGRATED FIRE CONTROL

30mm CHAIN GUN CANNON

TARGET ACQUISITION DESIGNATION SIGHT (TADS)

- Stabilized Sight for Day and Night Target Acquisition
- Azimuth ±120°
- Elevation +30° to -60°
- Slue Rate 60°/sec
- Day Side
  - - Direct View Optics
  - - Day TV
  - - Laser
- Night Side FLIR

ARMAMENT INTEGRATION

Ultimately, the effectiveness of any attack depends on the accuracy and destructive force of the firepower loosed against a target.

The sensor package makes it possible for the copilot/gunner to acquire super vision and scan long distances in limited visibility conditions, in safety. This is possible because the Apache can be operated at ranges beyond the kind of defenses anticipated in this kind of engagement and still see perfectly. In fog or light rain or when the target is obscured by smoke or dust, the FLIR sensor's ability to sight a "hot spot" greatly improves target recognition. Where color cues are important, the direct view system can be switched to four times or 16 times magnification. All optics in the TADS are stabilized to eliminate jumping images or jitter should the helicopter bounce around or vibrate for any reason.

Head-down on the optical relay tube of his TADS, the copilot has a high quality presentation of the television or FLIR images or a direct view through the optics. All the controls he needs to acquire, track, designate and fire on selected targets are mounted on hand grips on the side of the optical relay tube. In an attack, the target is first designated (spot illuminated) by an invisible laser beam, a nearly instantaneous event which measures the range for the FCC to direct weapons delivery. Range computations are needed for 70mm rockets and 30mm cannon fire. The laser guidance system in a HELLFIRE missile homes in on a specific target illuminated by a laser beam. As noted, in the hand-off mode, the target can be designated by another laser independent of the attacking Apache. Among other aids to targeting for a high probability of a first shot hit, the copilot/gunner can use automatic tracking by inserting moveable electronic "gates" over the target. The gates compensate for the helicopter moving rapidly from the point where the sighting began. Other refinements in the fire control system to allow for changing conditions during an attack include: linear motion compensation; offset tracking (whereby an imaginary target adjacent to the primary target can be designated and tracked so that the primary target is not aware it is being tracked); and indirect tracking, where the copilot/gunner looks at the scene through the direct view optics while the television or FLIR automatically tracks the target.

HELLFIRE

The HELLFIRE (AGM-114) laser-guided missile, the primary weapon aboard the AH-64A Apache at standoff ranges, can defeat the heaviest tanks currently operating throughout the world. HELLFIRE has a much shorter engagement time than earlier wire-guided missiles and can be launched from concealed positions. The missile can be launched in direct or indirect modes with single fire, rapid fire and/or ripple fire modes. In direct and rapid fire modes the Apache's on-board laser is used to designate the target. Ripple and indirect fire modes are used in "cooperative" attacks where targets are designated by other helicopters with laser designators, remotely piloted vehicles (RPVs), or designators carried by ground observers. In indirect firing, Apache can remain masked the entire time the missile is in flight from launch to target impact. This enhances survival and allows the crew to multiply their effectiveness by rapidly passing from target to target.

HELLFIRE's warhead consists of a powerful 17-pound, 7-inch diameter conical, shaped charge, designed to burn through the heavy armor found on the most modern

tanks. At launch, the missile is lofted under its own rocket power and descends towards its target at a steep angle in order to explode on the upper surfaces where a heavy tank is most vulnerable. In indirect fire, the missile can be launched either in a high trajectory to allow for terrain; for example, high angle firing over a hill, or in a lower trajectory where the cloud ceiling is low.

In the rapid fire mode, two or more missiles can be launched in quick succession, each homing on a common laser spot. As soon as the first missile strikes its target, the laser designating the first target is swung to the next target causing the remaining missiles in flight to alter their course to the next laser spot. This procedure is repeated until all missiles launched in the sequence have impacted. Autonomous designation from the Apache, or remote designation may be used for rapid fire but only one designator is needed. Ripple fire, on the other hand, needs two or more designators, each operating on a unique laser pulse frequency code and designating a different target. Prior to ripple firing, each of the missiles is given the electronic code of a particular designator, thereby tuning each missile seeker to a discrete target. This permits two or more missiles to be launched almost simultaneously at completely separate targets without the missiles confusing the targets on which they are to impact.

This flexibility in targeting and fire power, in conjunction with a sufficient number of remote designators, makes it possible for a single Apache to engage an entire tank column, almost simultaneously, without ever having to expose itself. With only two designators, each set to a different code, a ripple pair can be fired in rapid sequence approximately every eight seconds. This adds up to 16 HELLFIRE missiles fired against 16 separate targets in less than one minute. By comparison, only two or three TOW or HOT wire guided missiles could be fired during a comparable period of time and at much shorter range.

The identical type of HELLFIRE carried by Apache in the air-to-ground role, can also be used in air-to-air engagements for defense against other helicopters. Apache achieves this secondary role without having to preload dual stores, with separate missiles: one for air-to-air and one for antiarmor.

BATTLE TACTICS
I. AUTONOMOUS LAUNCH

II. RIPPLE FIRE LAUNCH

III. RAPID FIRE LAUNCH

61

70MM FFAR

The 70mm folding fin aerial rocket (FFAR) has been enhanced by fitting a new motor and multi-purpose warhead. This new rocket, especially when fired from the articulating pylons on the Apache, is significantly more effective than earlier versions. Up to 19 rockets each can be carried on four launchers; two on each stub wing for a total of 76. The mix of HELLFIRE missiles and aerial rockets carried aboard Apache is selected and loaded before flight to match the engagement. FFARs are used tactically against targets such as aircraft on the ground, troops, personnel carriers, ammunition storage areas, fuel tanks and radar equipment.

FFARs can be fired with aiming and steering commands shown on crew members' helmet displays or the copilot/gunner can use TADS for increased accuracy. Aiming information and fuse set data are provided by the mission equipment package. Functions of the aerial rocket control subsystem include:
• Fuse setting for range or tree height.
• Providing data to the Fire Control Computer for setting fuse times.
• Control of the launching mode: singles, pairs, quads or salvos.
• Control of the time intervals between launches.
• Launcher selection to maintain the balance of the aircraft laterally.
• Display of the quantities of rockets remaining.

Three optional rocket firing modes are available:
<u>Precision mode</u>: the pilot selects and fires the rockets, with the copilot/gunner using TADS. Aiming and steering commands for the helicopter are displayed on the pilot's helmet display. In all modes, fire control corrections are applied by the Fire Control Computer.
<u>Prime mode</u>: the pilot selects and fires rockets using his helmet display for aiming and steering.
<u>Backup mode</u>: the copilot/gunner fires rockets selected by the pilot. The copilot/gunner uses his helmet display for aiming and steering.

This outline of the Apache's three weapons systems shows how the two-man crew, using sensors to find and acquire targets under the most difficult conditions, can smoothly select the combination of firepower needed. Throughout the entire weapons selection and delivery operation, the man/machine interface functions for the most part unseen, other than the graphics on the crew displays. All three weapons are directed through the fire control computer, significantly enhancing the probability of hitting a target. The result is significant. By pre-pointing weapons and computing precise ballistic trajectories, the fire control computer reduces the time it takes to acquire targets and provides the best weapons systems performance ever achieved in an attack helicopter. Complete rearming and refueling in less than ten minutes in forward battle areas keeps the helicopter in the air. Apache's ability to battle by day or night and in adverse weather, multiplies the achievement.

AH-64A APACHE ATTACK HELICOPTER

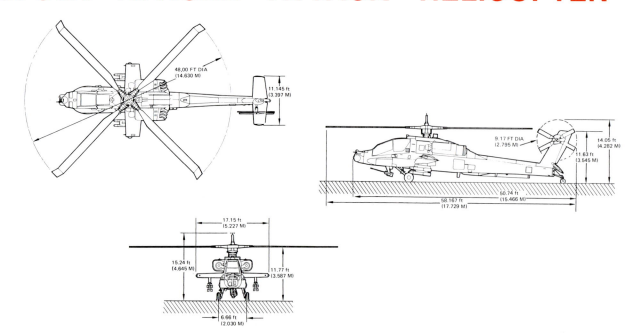

AH-64A Performance @ Primary Mission Gross Weight		
	Standard Day	**95°F**
Hover-In-Ground Effect (IRP)	15,000 Feet	10,200 Feet
Hover-Out-Of-Ground Effect (IRP)	11,500 Feet	7,000 Feet
Twin Engine Service Ceiling (IRP)	21,000 Feet	10,300 Feet
Single Engine Service Ceiling (IRP)	10,800 Feet	6,400 Feet
	Sea Level—Standard	**4,000 Feet/95°F**
Vertical Rate of Climb—FPM (IRP)	2,460	1,450
Maximum Rate of Climb—FPM (IRP)	3,200	2,570
Maximum Level Flight Speed—KTAS (IRP)	160▲	155
Cruise Speed—KTAS (@ MCP)	160▲	145
V_{DL} (Design Limit Speed)—KTAS	197	197
Maximum Range, Internal Fuel—NMi	260*	280*
Design Mission Endurance—Hour	2.63	1.83
Maximum Endurance; Internal Fuel—Hour	3.1	3.3

*30 Minute Reserve

▲ Trans. Limit

Weapons Capability

Weapons Load Capability:
- Hellfire Missiles ... 16
- 70mm Aerial Rockets ... 76
- 30mm Ammunition, Rounds ... 1,200

Engines (two each) T700-GE-701 Turboshaft ... 1694 SHP Each
One Engine Inoperative ... 1723 SHP

Weights:
- Weight Empty (actual) ... 10,760 Pounds
- Primary Mission Gross Weight ... 14,445 Pounds
- Ferry Mission (1,000 nautical miles) Gross Weight ... 21,000 Pounds

Dimensions:
- Main Rotor Diameter ... 48.0 Feet
- Tail Rotor Diameter ... 9.17 Feet
- Overall Length (Rotor Turning) ... 58.167 Feet
- Maximum Height (to top of air data sensor) ... 15.24 Feet
- Fuselage Width (at engine nacelles) ... 9.05 Feet
- Wing Span ... 17.15 Feet

**AH-64A APACHE
30mm Area Weapon
System**

The 30mm M230 automatic cannon is an area weapon carried primarily to provide suppressive fire. Firing dual purpose, linkless ammunition at 600 rounds a minute from a 1,200 round magazine, it is capable of destroying targets out to 4,000 meters. This makes the M230 a deadly threat to light vehicles and deployed infantry.

The gun is mounted in a remotely controlled chin turret, directed through the fire control system, makeing it very flexible in operation, even for self-protection against other helicopters. Should Fire Control Computer (FCC) corrections be unavailable, the gun can be fired from the fixed forward (stowed) position. In most cases, the M230 is operated by the copilot/gunner using the Target Acquisition Designation Sight (TADS) but can also be aimed by either crew member using his helmet- mounted sight. Sighting is exceptionally easy. The crew member only has to look at the target and the M230 tracks to his line of sight, ready for firing.

McDonnell Douglas Helicopter Company (then Hughes Helicopters) designed the single-barrel M230 around their externally powered Chain Gun (R) concept. This very successful innovation, with an electrically driven chain and sprocket rotating bolt mechanism, eliminated shock loads and low reliability inherent in self-powered guns. Low weight and smooth operation, with low failure rates, are the hallmarks of the Chain Gun concept.

The M230 can fire the M788 (TP) practice round, M789 (HEDP) high-explosive, dual-purpose round, M799 (HE) high-explosive round and NATO standard ADEN/DEFA 30mm ammunition. The ability of the turret to swing 110 degrees in azimuth on each side of the fuselage center line, pivot down 60 degrees and up 11 degrees, provides a very flexible, accurate field of fire over a broad area . Accurate aim and small dispersion result in a high hit probability. This accuracy together with the lethality of the 30mm round enable the M230 to fire at an efficient rate and for longer duration than earlier guns that depend on high rates of fire and wide dispersion to achieve the same results.

AH-64A 30 mm Area Weapon System

System Weight (Total)..................................1509 lb
System Weight (Empty)................................585 lb
Ammunition Capacity (M789)...........................1200 rnds
Rate of Fire...625 25 spm
Ammunition Handling System..................Linear Linkless

30mm M230 Area Weapon Characteristics

Caliber...30mm
Type...Externally Powered
Ammunition
  U.S. Combat................................. M789(HEDP), M799(HE)
  U.S. Practice..M788(TP)
  European......................................ADEN/DEFA(all)
Velocity... 2,650 ft/sec
Weight
  Receiver(includes motor)............................ 84 lb(38 kg)
  Barrel(42 in.)..................................... 32 lb(14.5 kg)
  Recoil Adapters.....................................11 lb(5.0 kg)
  Total Gun Weight.........................127 lb(57.5 kg)
  Linkless Transfer Unit..................... 8 lb(3.6 kg)
Dimensions
  Length................................. 66.0 in. (1676 mm)
  Width................................... 10.5 in. (267 mm)
  Height.................................. 11.4 in. (290 mm)
Barrel Life...................................10,000 rounds
Rate-of fire...................................... 625 ± 25 spm
Time-to-rate...0.2 sec
Time-to-stop.. 0.1 sec
Clearing Method................................... open bolt
Dispersion.. < 2 mil
Power Required... 3.0 hp
Reliability....................................15,000 MRBF

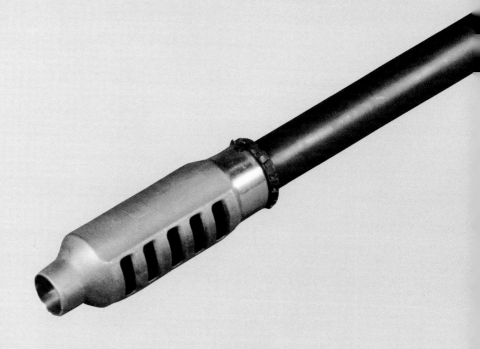

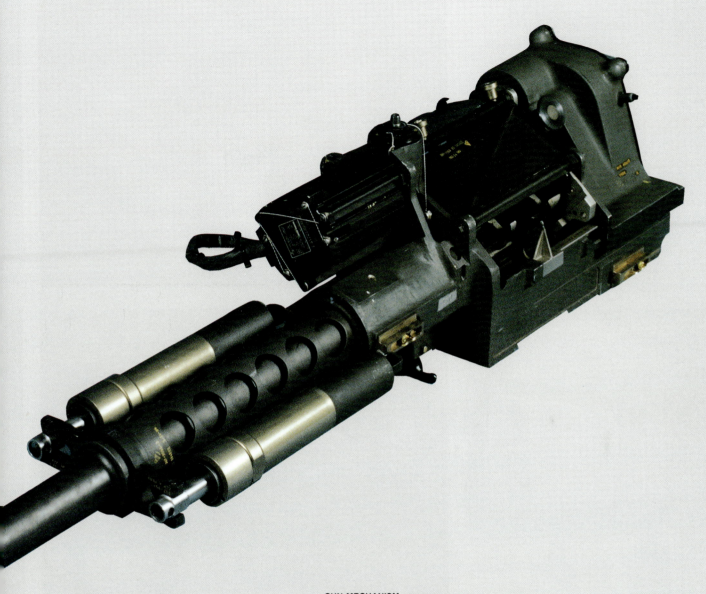

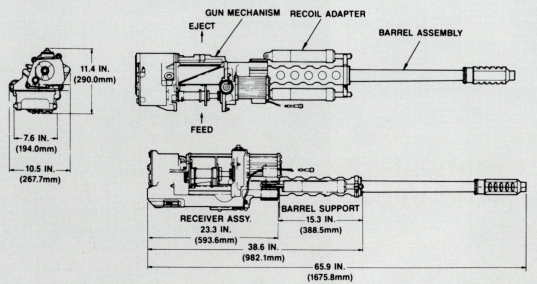

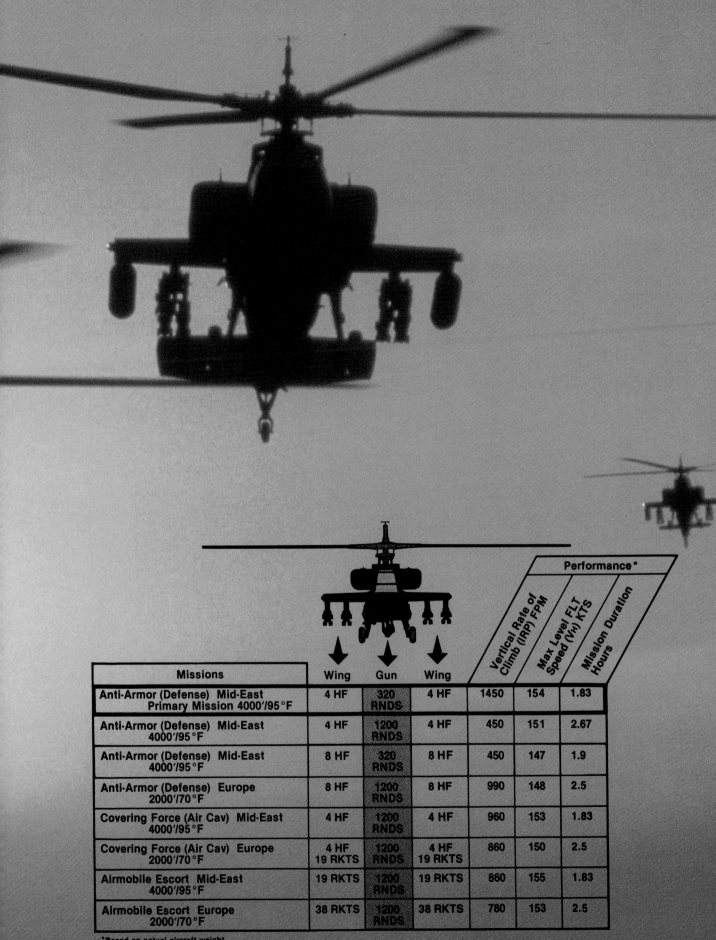

Missions	Wing	Gun	Wing	Vertical Rate of Climb (IRP) FPM	Max Level FLT Speed (V$_H$) KTS	Mission Duration Hours
Anti-Armor (Defense) Mid-East Primary Mission 4000'/95°F	4 HF	320 RNDS	4 HF	1450	154	1.83
Anti-Armor (Defense) Mid-East 4000'/95°F	4 HF	1200 RNDS	4 HF	450	151	2.67
Anti-Armor (Defense) Mid-East 4000'/95°F	8 HF	320 RNDS	8 HF	450	147	1.9
Anti-Armor (Defense) Europe 2000'/70°F	8 HF	1200 RNDS	8 HF	990	148	2.5
Covering Force (Air Cav) Mid-East 4000'/95°F	4 HF	1200 RNDS	4 HF	960	153	1.83
Covering Force (Air Cav) Europe 2000'/70°F	4 HF 19 RKTS	1200 RNDS	4 HF 19 RKTS	860	150	2.5
Airmobile Escort Mid-East 4000'/95°F	19 RKTS	1200 RNDS	19 RKTS	860	155	1.83
Airmobile Escort Europe 2000'/70°F	38 RKTS	1200 RNDS	38 RKTS	780	153	2.5

*Based on actual aircraft weight

AH-64 FIREPOWER
OPTIONS = MISSION FLEXIBILITY

TRAINING AND MAINTAINABILITY

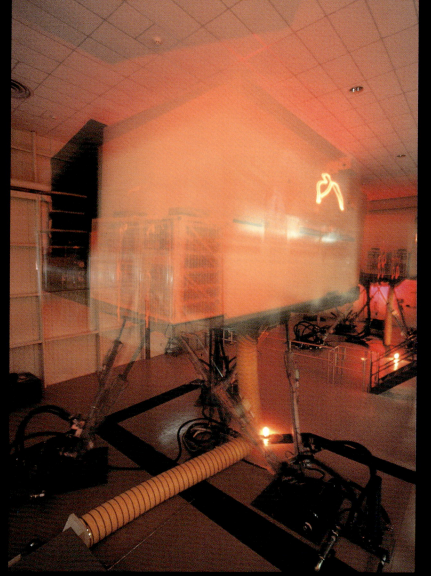

Skills are honed by pilots and ground crews undergoing highly specialized training to keep Apache combat ready.

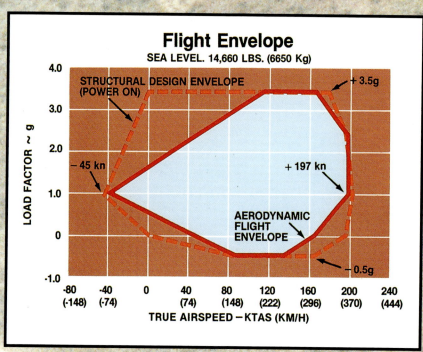

Flight Envelope
SEA LEVEL. 14,660 LBS. (6650 Kg)

Aircrew Training. The training program for the Apache was developed to transition qualified rotary wing pilots to an aircraft that is considerably more complex than its predecessors while permitting them to adapt to its new mission equipment package. In addition to standard classroom training, a Cockpit Weapons and Emergency Procedures Trainer (CWEPT) was built to introduce the two-man crew to the complexities of the mission equipment package, without leaving the ground. A second device, the Optical Relay Tube Trainer, is used to acquaint the copilot/gunner with the Target Acquisition Designations Sensor (TADS), of which the optical relay tube is a part. Both devices combine realistic hardware with simulation software to provide aircrew training at both primary and advanced levels. Crews learn correct cockpit procedures and, through simulation, become familiar with the symbols and controls on their displays. The practical result of simulation is that new crew members can reduce the time needed to make effective use of the live helicopter.

Simulation is not only effective in familiarizing crews with complex machines, it can also introduce critical "failures" into otherwise routine operations, at no risk to pilot or machine -- and at much lower cost than actually flying. Actual flight hours are reduced by "flying" a Combat Mission Simulator (CMS) that provides real time training of both crew members in all aspects of aircraft and weapon system operation. Night flying and adverse weather are part of the simulation. Because combat mission simulation is very effective for recurrent training, seven combat simulators will be built to keep Apache air crews right up to the mark; four are located in the U.S. and three at bases in Europe.

Individual pilot training is carried out at the Army Aviation Center at Fort Rucker, Alabama. It takes approximately 10 weeks and 45 flight hours to transition a qualified Army helicopter pilot into the Apache. Additional flight time is devoted to pilots destined to become instructors and maintenance test pilots; the latter continue training at Fort Eustis, Virginia, the center for maintenance training. Unit training begins at Fort Hood, Texas under the care of the Apache Training Brigade and continues in the field. All Apache units, including the National Guard, must successfully complete a "final exam" before being deployed.

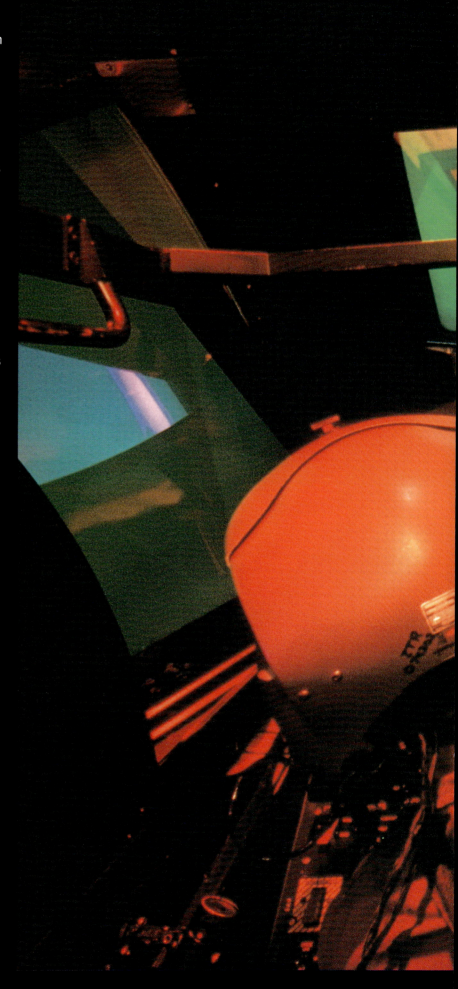

Maintenance training. Maintenance training follows much the same concept as pilot training, with standard classroom techniques augmented by sophisticated hands-on devices. Weapons, airframe, systems and maintenance training is performed at Fort Eustis, Virginia and avionics training at Fort Gordon, Georgia. The most impressive of the hands-on training devices is the composite trainer, essentially an all-up Apache (less weapons) that can do everything but fly. Similarly, there is a trainer for flight controls; one for the power train; an engine and auxiliary power unit trainer; two integrated avionics trainers; and an armament, fire control, and visionics trainer. Each device reproduces complete systems with all of the components installed that have to be maintained. In this way, a trainee can remove and install components as if he were working on an operational Apache. By linking computers to the trainers, instructors can deliberately insert faults that duplicate the real life readouts of an event. This allows students to hone their diagnostic skills in realistic trouble shooting drills.

In addition to complex hardware trainers, classroom systems panels have been developed to represent the hydraulic system, electrical power and distribution, pressurized air, fuel, mission equipment, digital automatic stabilization, on-board fault detection, and anti-icing. These panel trainers use computers, as in the hardware trainers, to allow instructors to insert faults for trainees to isolate, identify and correct. Once a trainee specialist completes his course and is confronted with actual problems on a real helicopter, he finds he is working on something with which he is already familiar; it looks the same, works the same, and is mounted in exactly the same position as the trainer.

Training at the aviation unit maintenance (AVUM) level and the aviation intermediate (AVIM) level is divided into 12 different specialties with standard skill level splits. This training is divided into courses that range from two to nine weeks of instruction depending on complexity.

ACCESSIBILITY

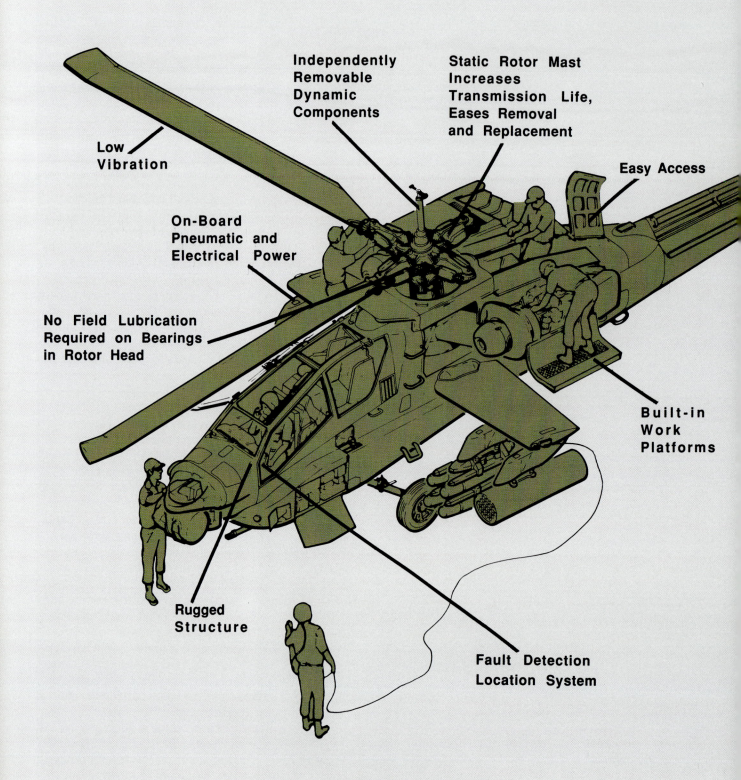

Sealed Grease Packed Gear Boxes

MAINTAINABILITY

The Apache was designed to be maintained by a front-line, Army field mechanic at a lower maintenance manhour per flight hour ratio than any previous attack helicopter. In current daily operation, Apache has been kept fully operational with 4.1 maintenance manhours per flight hour, compared with the specification requirement of no more than 13 manhours per flight hour. Availability, the other sensitive measure of maintenance support, is also running better than specification. Two battalions of Apaches during the last REFORGER exercises in Germany, a realistic measure of field conditions, were available 85% of the time, compared with the specification requirement of 70%.

Several features are designed into the Apache to make maintenance easier in the field. There are built-in maintenance platforms, quick-removal fairings, and large removable panels to provide easy access to internal components. The main transmission can be removed without pulling the main rotor or flight controls. Typical low-maintenance design features include the intermediate and tail rotor gearboxes that are lubricated with grease and a rotor head that requires no servicing. The tail rotor shaft uses two short and two long interchangeable segments, with flexible titanium couplings that do not require servicing. One mechanic can do most of the work to remove and replace the engine nose gearboxes.

Apache availability and mission reliability are supported by three levels of maintenance support: the user in the field (AVUM), intermediate (AVIM), and depot maintenance. There is a high degree of automated testing at each level. Maintenance downtime is lowered by the use of Line Replaceable Units (LRUs). In the event of a system failure, defective LRUs, identified by on-board automated testing, are easily removed and the system restored to operating condition by installing replacement units. Defective or suspected LRUs are sent to the intermediate maintenance organization for diagnostic tests and repair. LRUs are designed for easy testing without having to take them apart to access test points.

Apache has an on-board Fault Detection and Location System (FD/LS) that isolates faults to the LRU level. FD/LS can check out electrical or electronic subsystems in the air or on the ground. This system makes it possible to identify a very high percentage of all failures down to the particular faulty LRU, before, during or after a mission. A keyboard at the copilot/gunner's station is used to enter commands for FD/LS systems tests. Faults and their locations show up as alphanumeric displays on the TADS screen. During flight the FD/LS automatically monitors the operation of the mission equipment package and alerts the crew of malfunctions.

At the intermediate level (AVIM), defective LRUs removed from the aircraft are diagnosed and repaired by replacing electronic component boards (cards), using automatic test equipment mounted in mobile vans. Units and cards that cannot be repaired at the intermediate level are sent up the line to the depot; rebuilt units go back into inventory for issue to units in the field. When replacement LRUs are installed on the Apache, they are simply plugged in. There is no need to calibrate or adjust the system.

A high level of confidence is maintained in the helicopter by using the on-board test systems to constantly monitor system performance. This permits the use of "on-condition" maintenance, which means that many parts are replaced only when they show signs of wear. Before on-condition maintenance was introduced, many perfectly sound components were removed because they had reached an often arbitrary number of flight hours. On-condition means that a component can run close to its full service life. This practice lowers costs by reducing unnecessary maintenance.

Apache has brought several new dimensions to Army maintenance and training. It is no accident that Apache is the most reliable and maintainable attack helicopter ever developed.

DESIGNED FOR REDUCED MAINTENANCE

- Fewer Parts
- Fewer Inspections
- Longer Component Life
- Greater Availability
- Fewer Maintenance Manhours per flight hour
- Minimum Special Tool Requirements
- Easy Access to All Major Components
- Built-In Work Platforms
- Built-In Test Fault Detection Location System

APACHE MULTI-STAGE IMPROVEMENT PROGRAM

The AH-64A Apache Attack Helicopter flying today represents a great improvement over earlier attack helicopters. Progress in all phases of engineering design, however, did not stop with the AH-64A production. The Apache Multi-Stage Improvement Program (MSIP) aims at advancing Apache's capabilities in measured steps to upgrade existing capabilities and provide new features. These changes respond to threats expected to emerge in the 1990s and early in the next century that will impact helicopter operations. New missions such as deep strikes, in which units cross the Forward Line of Troops (FLOT), and air-to-air helicopter engagements are anticipated. Because the AH-64A is already successful as a weapons platform, with performance exceeding Army specifications, the bulk of MSIP changes are related to the mission equipment package. McDonnell Douglas Helicopter Company and team members on the program have been working towards an Advanced Apache by investing in independent research and development funds over the last several years. This effort was augmented by government funding of $25 million in fiscal 1988. The Army has proposed additional funding in fiscal year 1989 and beyond to continue MSIP development.

While today's Apache represents a significant advancement in the state-of-the-art of helicopter design, potential adversaries have not been standing still. Warsaw Pact countries are introducing new weapons or upgrading existing systems, including the ZSU-X mobile cannon and portable ground-to-air missiles such as the SA-14 Gremlin. A series of attack helicopters have also emerged, including the Mi-24 Hind, Mi-28 Havoc, and KA-30 Hokum. Soviet technology is improving on many different fronts with improved radars, electro-optical jammers, acoustic detectors, and nuclear, biological and chemical threats. On the U.S. side, in addition to meeting changing threats and planning new missions there is a continuing drive to improve the reliability and maintainability of all systems as a way to lower operation and support costs.

Listed below are the major elements in the Multi-Stage Improvement Program currently envisioned for Apache:

- Airborne Adverse Weather Weapon System, a target acquisition and fire control system to provide fire-and-forget HELLFIRE capability that will substantially reduce target acquisition and engagement time lines in any weather.
- Improved Electromagnetic Vulnerability protection and hardening against the high electromagnetic pulses experienced in nuclear detonations.
- Upgraded cockpits with automated monitoring and control of routine aircraft functions for better crew and mission effectiveness.
- Improved Helmet Display Unit, to include image intensification for both pilots.
- Air-to-Air Enhancements, including air-to-air missiles and 30mm gun system improvements.
- Fire Control Computer provides faster processing, greater redundancy and built-in growth
- Larger forward avionics bays to house additional equipment.
- Laser protective visor to counter laser damage to the eyes.
- Increased electrical power with automated management.
- Navigation improvements with ring-laser gyros and "embedded" precision sensors that will obtain accurate positioning from Global Positioning System (GPS) satellites.
- Improved 1553B data bus architecture.
- Improved hover augmentation system.
- Improvements in the integration of the IR jammer, radar warning, radio frequency interference, missile warning, laser warning, and optical warning.
- Common engine program with the UH-60 Black Hawk series of helicopters.
- New environmental control and integrated pressurized air systems.

Current "mission expansion" on the Apache includes the Airborne Target Handover System (ATHS) using digital communications and the air-to-air STINGER missile for a greatly expanded air combat role. ATHS incorporates a number of advanced features that enhance combat efficiency and improve survivability by using digital data burst, anti-jamming and "no-voice" communications between the aircraft and ground stations.

These changes will make it possible for both the pilot and the copilot/gunner to access all communications and navigation equipment, and input the fire control system. This provides greater sharing of the workload, especially during hot combat, and keeps all systems functioning in case one of them is disabled. Other features include: the user data module and transfer system; remote frequency displays; doubling the volume available for future avionics, and provisions for the new single channel ground and airborne radio systems (SINCGARS).

The Multi-Stage Improvement Program is currently split into two parts: Stage I provides near term improvement to be fielded in 1993 to 1994 that will sustain Apache effectiveness until the year 2000. Stage II will add advanced technology to provide enhancements that will last well into the next century.

Advanced Apache Concept In Multi-Mission Role

Stage I also introduces the new Airborne Adverse Weather Weapon System (AAWWS); integrated cockpit controls and displays; a fully redundant data bus system; ADA, the new higher order language in the common computer operating program for military systems; and improvements in maintenance support. A Stage II program, now being considered for a start in the late 1990s, would look at advanced technology sensors, integrated sensor functions, new flight controls, and other new developments to bring an even higher level of automation to crew tasks.

The Apache that will emerge from the Multi-Stage Improvement Program will be an advanced air-to-air and air-to-ground aircraft with dramatically increased capabilities. The new technologies that improve and refine the mission equipment package also carry simple benefits in hidden places . For example, the number of black boxes will be cut in half yet the systems will have more redundancy, which lowers system failure rate while increasing survivability. The reduced number of electronic boxes will be smaller and weigh less, because they will incorporate more advanced integrated circuit technology. There will be greater commonality between boxes than before, making repairs easier. Standard wire bundles will be replaced in many places with new flat cables, with 35% fewer total wires yet higher redundancy. The new wiring system offering superior

electromagnetic protection can be replaced in modules. Advanced electronics will enter the maintenance orbit with built-in, self-test, continuous monitoring devices that will generate a data cassette output for analysis by maintenance crews. The monitoring system will also flag in-flight warnings to the crew. Improved operation and support features will lower maintenance costs by 15% from the basic AH-64A.

The two-man crews flying MSIP Apaches will have such a high degree of automation at their fingertips that they will be able to monitor missions, using the concept of "management by exception", rather than handling every detail. The "glass cockpit" with integrated, touch-screen color displays, as well as alphanumeric keypads for inputting data, will greatly simplify crew tasks and reduce workload considerably. Less work in the cockpit and refined multi-mission weapons such as the fire-and-forget HELLFIRE and air-to-air STINGER will make it possible for Apache to do more things better. Apache is already the most effective attack helicopter in the world. Tomorrow's Apache, with the MSIP refinements added to the proven platform, will carry the machine well into the 21st century.

As part of its Advanced Apache program, McDonnell Douglas Helcopter Company is exploring a shipboard version of Apache to protect ocean vessels sailing without carrier air cover. Naval Apache, as currently proposed, would have a 200 nautical mile mission radius with four hours on station, carrying a mix of antiship and air-to-air weapons.

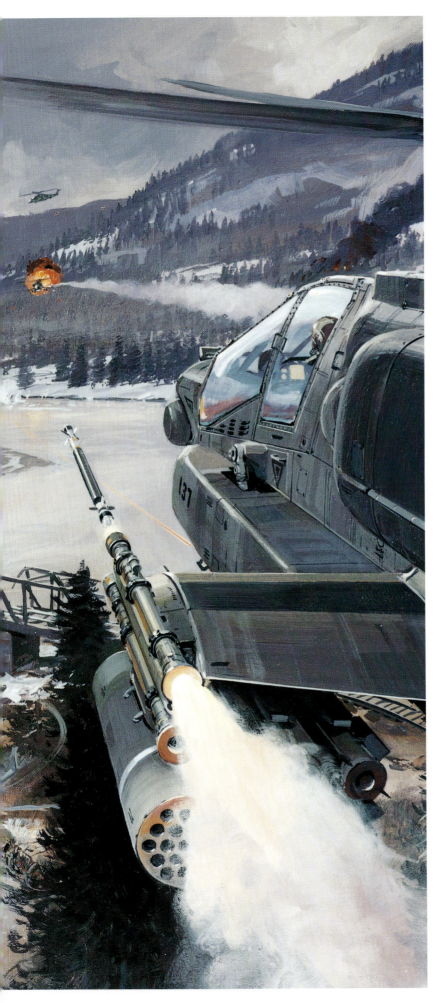

AIR-TO-AIR STINGER (ATAS)

Defensive air combat is a secondary mission for Apache that will begin with the Air-to-Air STINGER (ATAS). ATAS is a derivative of the very effective Man Portable Anti-Aircraft Defense System (MANPADS) missile introduced in the early 1970s. STINGER's infrared guidance system makes it possible to fire and forget. Once STINGER has been aimed at a target then fired, the missile automatically tracks the target until impact. The many years of experience with the MANPADS STINGER, during which thousands of rounds were produced and a huge number fired, is built into ATAS. Improved air-to-air Apache will mount two STINGER launchers, one on the tip of each stub wing; each launcher carries two missiles for a maximum weapon load of four STINGERs. The ATAS launchers may be jettisoned in an emergency.

A single ATAS launcher loaded with two missiles weighs only 103 pounds. The round used for helicopters is identical to those already in volume production for air defense. High rate production translates into low cost per missile. Missiles are stored as dead rounds and need no maintenance; built-in test checks out the system aboard the aircraft.

ATAS does not intrude into Apache's primary antiarmor role or conflict with the way the helicopter is operated. ATAS is also easy to operate. Once the target is located, the missile system is activated and the helicopter maneuvered to position the target within the missile seeker field of regard. The missile seeker can be directed to the target by the pilot or copilot/gunner using the helmet mounted display (IHADSS) or the copilot/gunner using the TADS. Once target lock-on is verified by an acquisition tone and display symbology, the missile can be fired leaving Apache free to engage another target or begin evasive maneuvers. Once a missile is fired, the system automatically sequences the next missile to engage a second target.

During the formal development and operational test (DT/OT) evaluation for the Army, in daylight and at night from a helicopter, ATAS was launched 12 times and scored eight hits; four of the 12 firings were scored as "no-tests". ATAS logged 510 flight test hours during DT/OT and is reported to have experienced only one failure that would affect an air-to-air mission. Air-to-air STINGER is now in production and will be fielded in 1989.

Apache Achieves Army's Goals From Development to Deployment

"We have the dawning of a new era. We have the mobility and firepower differential that makes a smart enemy sweat, and a less intelligent one die for his country."
Quote by Lt. Gen. Crosbie E. Saint when commanding the US Army, III Corps, Fort Hood, Texas.

Modern weapons systems take years to mature from concept to deployment. In the case of the Apache Attack Helicopter, 14 years stretch from the start of research and development in 1972 to 1986, when the first Apache Attack Battalion achieved initial operating capability. Full-scale production began in late 1982. Because the nature of a threat and the technology to counter it can change radically during a long development cycle, users and makers stretch to their limits to avoid obsolescence before their creation is fielded. Design, manufacture, training, and myriad hidden facets come together in deployment, where the success of the system is measured in the real world.

The following key points were the original objectives in the Apache program. The new helicopter had to have superior performance, carry multiple firepower options, assure 24-hour bad weather capability, and be reliable, maintainable, survivable, responsive and affordable.

They add up to the effective multi-mission tank killer being deployed today in large numbers at home and abroad. Apache is a success because of the practical vision of the Army from the beginning and the technical merit of the Apache design and production teams.

The first production AH-64A Apache was delivered to Fort Eustis, Virginia in January 1985. In October 1985 the 50th production Apache was delivered and by July 1986 the first combat unit, the 3rd Squadron, 6th Cavalry Regiment, was qualified as combat ready at Fort Hood, Texas. By July 1988, seven Apache battalions had been fielded.

The U.S. Army has contingency plans that range from a minimum force of 863 Apaches to 1,031 Apaches in 47 combat battalions. Each battalion in the force structure currently planned contains from 15 to 18 AH-64A Apaches, backed by a mix of 13 OH-58 Kiowa scout helicopters and 3 UH-60 Black Hawk utility helicopters. A typical battalion consists of 21 officers, 44 warrant officers and 199 enlisted personnel. This battalion normally operates a fleet of 6 utility vehicles, 7 tankers, and 42 cargo trucks, giving some idea of the mobility of just one battalion.

In the fiscal budgets through 1989, 675 aircraft have been authorized. This budget authority would take production deliveries through calendar 1991. To achieve a procurement of 1,031 aircraft, follow-on production of additional AH-64As, under a proposed multi-year procurement offering considerable savings, would seem likely. The ultimate disposition of a 1,031 buy would see 689 aircraft in the active battalions, 270 in the National Guard, and 72 in the Army Reserve. This level of procurement extends production into 1996. As in any other massive program, the actual numbers procured are subject to interpretations of need and Congressional sentiments.

Apaches roll off the line at the McDonnell Douglas Helicopter's Mesa, Arizona facility.

The Army adopted a single-station unit fielding and training concept in which all Apaches enter service through the III Corps, Apache Training Brigade at Fort Hood, Texas. From there, Apaches can easily be flown from base to base within the U.S. on internal fuel. Where longer range is needed, such as in overseas deployments, auxiliary tanks can be installed on the stub wings to achieve a ferry range of 800 nautical miles with a 20 minute reserve. Rapid strategic deployment uses U.S. Air Force airlift capacity. A single Apache can be carried in a C-130; two in a C-141B; three in the future C-17; and six in a C-5A. It takes seven loaders six hours to prepare and stow six Apaches aboard the C-5A. Unloading is a simple reversal of the loading process.

In January 1988, the 2nd Squadron, 6th Cavalry was assigned to USAREUR and stationed in Illesheim as part of the 11th Aviation Brigade, VII Corps. This unit had already participated in the Fall REFORGER exercise.

Another notable milestone was achieved, when in May 1988 an Apache logged the 100,000th flight hour for the entire production fleet. Two more squadrons are scheduled for deployment to Europe by the end of 1988. The Army plans to attach three Apache battalions to each Army corps, while each division will receive two AH-64A battalions.

The most reliable observations on any system come from users. This overview of Apache concludes with several comments by users. They are the men who know the aircraft and its weapons intimately.

Lt. Gen. Crosbie E. Saint, Commander of III Corps and Fort Hood, commenting on REFORGER '87 to the Killeen (Texas) Herald in October 1987.
"The Apache greatly surprised a lot of our allies who thought we were just blowing smoke. The Apache squadrons performed wonderfully. They should be proud of themselves."

Lt. Gen. Ronald L. Watts, Commanding General, VII Corps, on first deployment in Europe.
"Deployment of this squadron signals a significant change in VII Corps' ability to carry the fight to the enemy, should deterrence fail. The Apache helicopter is one of the most important fighting vehicles I have in the Corps. Unhindered by terrain, designed to fight day or night, the AH-64 adds a lethal unit and a new dimension to the Corps' fighters."

And finally, an Apache pilot, CW2 Paul Deaner, talking to Soldiers Magazine, March 1988.
"...it's 100 times more agile than the Cobra. It turns on a dime. Apache is faster, and because it has two engines, it's safer. It has 10 times more optic power than a Cobra. The way we are configured with Apaches and Kiowas and Black Hawks, I'd feel real confident going into battle."

Army personnel loading AH-64A Apache into C-5A transport.

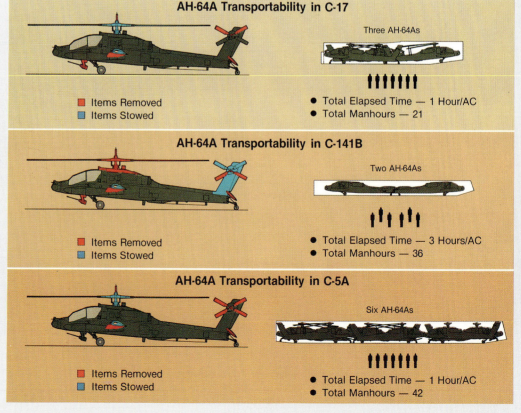

ILLUSTRATION BY JOHN BATCHELOR

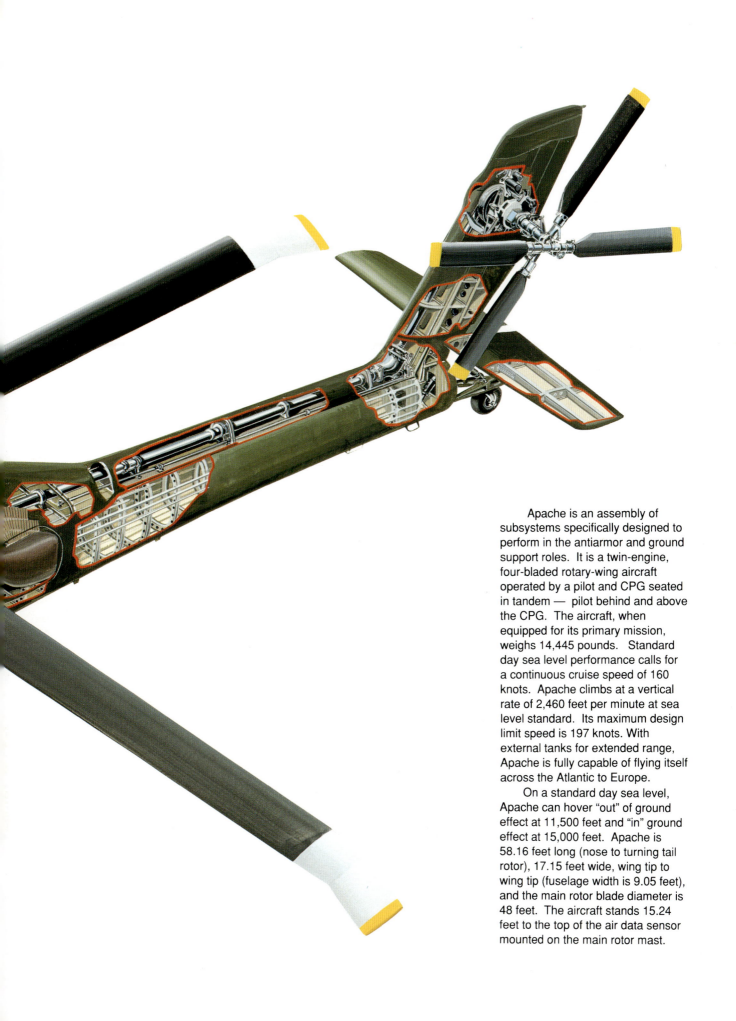

Apache is an assembly of subsystems specifically designed to perform in the antiarmor and ground support roles. It is a twin-engine, four-bladed rotary-wing aircraft operated by a pilot and CPG seated in tandem — pilot behind and above the CPG. The aircraft, when equipped for its primary mission, weighs 14,445 pounds. Standard day sea level performance calls for a continuous cruise speed of 160 knots. Apache climbs at a vertical rate of 2,460 feet per minute at sea level standard. Its maximum design limit speed is 197 knots. With external tanks for extended range, Apache is fully capable of flying itself across the Atlantic to Europe.

On a standard day sea level, Apache can hover "out" of ground effect at 11,500 feet and "in" ground effect at 15,000 feet. Apache is 58.16 feet long (nose to turning tail rotor), 17.15 feet wide, wing tip to wing tip (fuselage width is 9.05 feet), and the main rotor blade diameter is 48 feet. The aircraft stands 15.24 feet to the top of the air data sensor mounted on the main rotor mast.